Grandad

With love and Congra

90th Birthday

from

Christopher & Judith

x x x x

Trout and Salmon Fishing

A drift on Loch Assynt in Sutherland

TROUT & SALMON FISHING

Editor:
ROY EATON

David & Charles
Newton Abbot   London   North Pomfret (Vt)

British Library Cataloguing in Publication Data

Trout and salmon fishing
1. Salmon-fishing
2. Trout-fishing
I. Eaton, Roy
799.1'755   SH684

ISBN 0 7153 8117 2

First published 1981
Second impression 1984
Third impression 1985

Printed in Great Britain by
Redwood Burn Ltd, Trowbridge, Wilts.
for David & Charles Publishers Limited
Brunel House Newton Abbot Devon

Published in the United States of America
by David & Charles Inc
North Pomfret Vermont 05053 USA

Contents

Introduction   Roy Eaton   9

I FLIES

The colour of the day   L S Paterson   12
Meeting the challenge of the midge   John Poole   14
Imitation and presentation   Richard Walker   18
Silverhorns on the lake   J R Harris   24
March days on the Usk   Oliver Kite   32
The art of winging flies   Geoffrey Bucknall   34
Observations on chironomids   John Goddard   40
A team of loch flies   H A Oatts   44
Confidence in flies   Frederick Mold   48
Dealing with dimplers   C R Pearce   50
Black magic for blank days   Francis Harmar   54
Stoneflies for trout   G A Grattan   57

II TROUT

The late starter   J H Foy   63
That old Test magic   Gordon Carlisle   66
Sunshine/shadow strategy   C R Pearce   70
When a loch is dour   'Alexandra'   74
Bad weather in spring   C R Pearce   79
A theory of light   Frederick Mold   82
Learn to cast a long line   Richard Walker   84

Trouting in moorland streams · B W C Cooke · 88
Loch Tay on a day in spring · Peter Reid · 90
Irish trout on salmon flies · Dermot Wilson · 94
A dilemma of reservoir trouting · F W Holiday · 100
Spring could be a little late this year · Bruce Sandison · 105
These long, hot days of summer · Peter Lapsley · 109
The Blagdon 'boil' · Conrad Voss Bark · 113
Learning by experience · Stanley Woodrow · 117
American trout · Hubert J Pepper · 121

III   GRAYLING

Do grayling really have soft mouths? · Donald Overfield · 129
How big do grayling grow? · T K Wilson · 133
Grayling under scrutiny · Oliver Kite · 136

IV   SEA TROUT

Fishing in the autumn · Moray McLaren · 143
The temperamental sea trout · Kenneth Dawson · 146
Sea trout from salt water · C R Pearce · 152

V   SALMON

When the river turns sour · David Barr · 157
Springers in the snow · Ian Wood · 160
Reflections on catching a salmon · Kenneth Dawson · 163
Twirling for salmon · J R Harris · 170
The gamble of the spate river · David Barr · 174
When I go fishing · Major-General R N Stewart · 177
The luck of the game · Kenneth Dawson · 182
Salmon or trout? · J D Brayshaw · 187
The frustrations of salmon fishing · Ian Niall · 191
November on Tweed · Arthur Oglesby · 194

CONTENTS

The light touch . . . when playing
  salmon   Douglas Iron   197
The Tay again   Ian Wood   202
Summer tactics on the Welsh Dee   S J Diggory   205
Thoughts on autumn salmon   G P R Balfour-
                                      Kinnear   209

Introduction

Since the first volume to bear the title *The Complete Trout and Salmon Fisherman* was published two years ago, *Trout and Salmon*, the magazine which gave it that title, has passed a notable milestone. It has celebrated its Silver Jubilee, twenty-five years of keeping the British game-fisherman abreast of developments in his sport, of news of what has been going on through the seasons on the rivers and lakes, of ways and means of increasing his success and enjoyment in his fishing, and simply of providing him with good reading with which to relax after a day at the waterside.

It has been an eventful quarter-century, and for trout-fishing especially one of great progress. The making of many new reservoirs and smaller still-waters and the coming of the rainbow trout has opened up the sport to many more thousands than followed it previously. For salmon-fishing it has been a more traumatic period, with stocks under threat from disease and netting, from pollution and poaching, yet it has ended with hope that better things may be to come.

The selection of articles from *Trout and Salmon* which makes up this new volume reflects all that and much more. It offers something for everyone—for the trout-fisher, for the salmon-fisher and for the fisher for sea trout, for the grayling-fisher and for the fly-tyer. And for those who are content simply to call themselves fishermen, it offers a whole lot more besides. This is a book to keep by you and to open at random at the end of the day, perchance to discover a morsel of knowledge that may make tomorrow better than its promise, or to induce a reverie of angling delight.

To paraphrase Howard Marshall in that very first issue of *Trout and Salmon* all those years ago, 'If it can rest, cheer and divert you with equally happy results, then we shall indeed be satisfied.'

July 1980   *Roy Eaton*

I
Flies

Flies

The colour of the day

As one who is not at all a believer in one particular pattern of fly or colour of spinning bait, but only in size and presentation, I must admit that there can be days on a particular river or loch when the fish are interested in only one offering.

I remember an outing on Loch Laidon just before the last war, when it turned out to be a 'yellow day'. Loch Laidon is a big, moorland water, the highest of the chain of lochs which link up to form the Rannoch Tummel river system. It is full of small trout, with a few large fish rarely hooked on fly.

Three of us fished. One was new to any kind of fishing, but was a cheerful, try-anything companion. He used borrowed tackle and produced a horrible-looking fly, a huge bushy thing, bright yellow, which a keeper had given him. We laughed at it, saying it was bigger than the mouths of the trout in Laidon, and, I added, bigger than some of the trout! Apart from John and his enormous yellow object, we were on the usually successful 12s and 10s.

All we were getting were trout so small that even on Loch Laidon we did not keep any. Then John, the beginner, hooked something much better and played it very well under our instruction. In the lunchtime we were convinced that it was the bright yellow colour that was bringing success. A frantic search in our well-stocked boxes yielded nothing that was all-yellow—and at the end of the day John had seven trout for $15\frac{1}{2}$lb and we had nothing worth taking back.

John stoutly refused to lend us his fly because of our previous remarks, and because it was becoming very battered. He finally lost the thing when a real monster broke him and went off with it and the cast. The day was bright, the sky cloudless, and the loch at low June level. After that, we always took some specially-dressed, big, bushy yellow flies to the loch—and never hooked anything on them.

On another occasion, on a Sutherland hill-loch above Strath

Halladale, it was a Kingfisher size 12 that had notable success, and again it was the only one in the fly-boxes we had in the boat. My wife got it, and kept to it, saying there were plenty more down in the car and it was only a mile downhill—and up again.

It was a hot day, and we morosely fished nearly everything else we had, but she had a fine catch, including three on at the same time, good fish, and all successfully netted. She stopped getting fish only when the hackle came off her now well-used fly. It was colour again, you see, obviously the orange of the hackle, and it was another bright day, with hardly any wind, which is unusual on any Sutherland loch at this height.

Blue was the colour on the Cam Loch, in southern Sutherland, one outing in July. I had a size 8 Blue Zulu on the bob, and it took all the trout that day. My companion rooted through all the fly-boxes and found, and tried, Teal, Blue and Silvers, Blue Charms and other blue patterns. But in none of them was the blue quite as vivid as that on the Zulu. Black Zulus of the same size brought no response, so it was clearly the shade of blue that was attractive on that day (dull, with an overcast sky and a soft south wind). On the Cam Loch it is most unusual for a Black Pennell or a Grouse and Claret to fail.

Even the stupid salmon can recognise a definite colour, and it is well known that in the short period of a low sun in the evening, a yellow fly often does well for salmon and grilse in summer, when the water is warm and the level is low. I was fishing the River Annan in Dumfriesshire, in August, in one of the years when there was an exceptionally good run of grilse. I thought I would try one of my favourites for such conditions, the Evening Glow, which is a mainly yellow fly, with a fluorescent yellow hackle, but couldn't find one. The only other predominantly yellow fly I could find was an old Goldfinch, size 4, which I thought was far too large for the conditions. However, on it went, and at once I was into a grilse. I had four more before the light faded, and my companion, who is a confirmed believer in hair-wing tube flies, persisted with a black-and-yellow and had only one fish on it, and nothing on any other colour.

13

Loch Leven produced a problem one day when we were caught in a terrific thunderstorm near the west end of St Serf's Island and had to sit out in drenching rain for half an hour. Then the sky cleared and a cooling breeze arrived. I had a garish-looking fly, a famous transatlantic pattern called the Parmachene Belle, and thought I would try it, in conditions which seemed hopeless.

I put it on the bob, and at once the trout started to take it—and nothing else on any of the three rods. I had a fine catch, but was it the scarlet or the white, or the combination of both on this red-and-white confection, which attracted them in these unusual atmospheric conditions? I have never hooked anything on the Belle since that day.

The last remembered instance of definite preference for a particular colour was on the Border Esk, on the Canonbie stretch. Grey was the colour of the day on this occasion, but perhaps this is not so remarkable, as the fly which did so well is a favourite on this famous sea-trout river. It was the Langholm Silver, a greyish fly, with a curlew wing, and in the evening it accounted for all the sea trout I caught, and all those hooked by my companion. Neither of us had an offer on any other pattern, though all of these were proven patterns for the Esk.

All this seems to show that fish will take an offering in a particular colour when conditions are just right—lighting, temperature, the water, and the way they are feeling at the time—and will reject anything else. Certainly I no longer number myself among the considerable number of anglers who think fish are colour-blind.

October 1974   *L. S. Paterson*

Meeting the challenge of the midge

One of the common calls from the still-water angler is 'you might as well pack up—they're midging'. This doom-laden appeal is usually heard on a warm, windless day when the water appears unusually silent and its glassy surface is being quietly and systematically knifed by a flotilla of dorsal fins as the trout roll lazily near the surface gorging on the hatching chironomids to the apparent exclusion of all else.

Many anglers succumb to what they believe is the inevitable and fail to regard this situation as a direct challenge.

'Waste of time,' one says. 'When they're midging, they'll look at nothing else.'

'I've tried them with everything down to size 18,' grumbles another. 'If they won't look at an 18 what can you do?'

This latter complaint is typical and stems from the far-too-commonly held assumption that as soon as midges are mentioned you should think only in terms of size 16 to 20 hooks. Nothing could be more wrong.

The midge family belongs to the largest, and for the still-water angler probably the most important, order of flies, the *Diptera*. There are thousands of species in this order, varying in size from the daddy-long-legs down to smuts and with bodies of every colour carried on your silk bobbins. Many of the *Diptera* are terrestrials, like the common house-fly, but the family of the order which matters most to the angler is that of the midges or *Chironomidae*. This family itself has hundreds of species, some of which are up to 1in long.

When the trout are midging, the first requirement is the same as for a hatch of duns. If you wish to fish the fly causing the action, you must first see what it looks like. Inability to identify the species by name is no serious handicap, as it doesn't prevent you noting the shape, size and colour of the creature, which is all the knowledge you require to tie on the best likeness you have. That puts you in with a better chance than simply selecting your tiniest dressing regardless, as many do.

There is, however, a better method, and that is to fish the midge pupa as you would the appropriate nymph during a movement of *Ephemeroptera*. Both are intermediate stages of the fully-developed fly. With the midges, the process is egg to larva to pupa to adult fly, whereas with the ephemerons it is egg to nymph to dun to spinner. During the hatch from pupa to adult midge, the trout feed just

15

as steadily under the surface as on top, whereas a fall of spinners, in my experience, induces only surface activity. This means that during a hatch the nymph or pupa concerned can be successfully fished at any depth consistent with the journey the insect makes to the surface for its metamorphosis, and in this respect I have had as much success with a sinking line as with a floater.

The first artificial midge pupa to achieve widespread praise was the Black Buzzer, credited to Dr Bell, of Blagdon fame. It is not known how he arrived at the dressing, but the possibility that the famous Clyde Blae and Black may have entered his thoughts cannot be ruled out. This fly is a good presentation of the black midge and the name 'Buzzer' is assumed to have originated from the buzzing sound emitted by many species of chironomids during flight. This, of course, is conjecture, but one thing is certain, the Black Buzzer has been followed by a host of other buzzers—red, green, brown, yellow—and the field is still wide open to experiment.

Buzzers are much easier to dress than standard flies, as they require no wings or hackles. There are, however, some points in their make-up which, I believe, benefit from a small degree of exaggeration, and these are the body segmentations, the thorax and the tracheal gills. The body segmentations are very distinct on the natural creature, and this physical feature can be pointed up by using wool instead of silk for the body dressing. The gilt or silver wire used in the ribbing should be a shade thicker than that used over silk, and tinselled thread would be best but for its vulnerability to hard-mouthed fish.

These materials bed down better in wool, and I have found that pure wool is much superior to nylon mixture in appearance and moisture absorbency. The thorax of many of the larger common midges can be shown, according to the species, by a couple of turns of either bronze peacock-herl, ostrich herl dyed brown or wound fibres from a white turkey-tail which has been stained with picric acid.

For the delicate tracheal gills I find the tips of white or cream cock-hackles to be best. They give excellent movement under water. A small bunch of fibres from the same hackle can, if desired, be tied

16

in at the tail to represent the tiny caudal fins which, though actually translucent, are very active and probably create minute currents which may be visible to the trout.

Last season I dressed four colours of pupae on hook sizes 10 and 12. They were intended to represent the black midge, the large red, the orange silver and the large green. The first to interest the trout were the Black Midge and the Orange Silver, which took fish throughout the season, including some rainbows over 3lb. The Red Midge was spasmodically successful, and the Green Midge a comparative failure, in spite of which I believe it is worth another season's trial.

The materials for dressing these buzzers are cheap and easy to come by. The wool should be four-ply pure wool and the colours are black, maroon, light orange and bright green. You must also have silk thread of the same colours as binders for the wool.

The method of dressing is simple. Wax the thread and wind it along the shank from eye to partly round the hook-bend. Tie in three or four fibres from the white cock-hackle and 2in of gilt or silver ribbing. Take a 5in length of the wool and separate the strands by pulling two apart in each hand then pulling one of the pairs apart. Tie in the single strand of wool at the tail, wind it along the shank to within ¼in of the eye, then back over itself towards the tail, ensuring a slight taper in thickness from eye to bend. Tie in the end of the wool with the thread, then wind the thread as a binder over the wool to the eye, and secure. Wind the ribbing towards the eye and secure with the thread. Tie in the hackle-tip so that it projects over the eye by ¼in. Tie in one strand of herl at the thorax and whip-finish in front of the hackle-tip. The Large Red, the Orange Silver and the Black Buzzer take peacock herl at the thorax, while the Large Green takes ostrich dyed brown. Although the size 10 hook approximates nearest to the actual size of the insect, the size 12 was accepted by about the same number of fish.

These dressings were fished in turn as singles on a 9ft leader, then in twos as point and one dropper on the same length leader, and finally as point and two droppers on leaders of 9ft to 12ft. This latter arrangement was the most successful, its greatest annoyance being the frequency of takes on the bob and middle dropper with consequent tangles in the landing-net.

The sport produced by these pupae has convinced me that the anglers who lump midging trout into the size 16 to 20 hook range—and I believe there are many of them—are losing out considerably, for there are just as many large species around as small. And as they are all taken the same way by the trout because of their common hatching process, the slow-rolling dorsal on the flat calm gives no clue whatever to the size of the midge causing the excitement. In view of this, the wails of despondency one hears at the waterside immediately the trout start on a midging spree are seldom, if ever, justified.

April 1974   *John Poole*

Imitation and presentation

On a recent expedition after trout, I met an able young man who deplored the use of a sunk fly on the grounds that it was too easy and therefore unsportsmanlike. The fishery concerned was a still-water one, where dry-fly fishing consists simply of casting out a water-proofed artificial and then sitting down to wait for a trout to come along and take it. It is not even necessary to cast very far.

In the same water, a sunken fly must be chosen to sink to the right depth, which must be judged. And when it has been cast and given the right time to sink, it must be given the right motion. All of which demands skills of judgment and of hand not required for fishing the floater.

That these relative skills may be reversed on a river—though that is by no means proven—matters not. Here was a young fellow who had had it drummed into his head—where it rested without disturbance by thought—that dry-fly fishing is more sportsmanlike than wet-fly fishing.

On the same water, but from an older angler, I heard this: 'I detest this sunken-nymph fishing—it teaches the trout to be bottom-feeders!' The thought immediately occurred to me that if nymph-fishing teaches the trout anything, it is surely to avoid bottom-feeding.

Then we have the presentation-alone school of thought. Present your artificial fly correctly, they say, and you will catch trout, no matter what sort of fly you use. In the broadest sense, they are right, though I fancy I could tie them some flies that would severely limit the numbers of trout they caught. In any waters, though, there are some trout that will take anything. You can sometimes drop them various inedible objects such as cigarette ends or pieces of silver paper, usually from bridges, and see them take and hold these objects long enough to allow hooking, were hooks present.

Anyone who lays down what trout won't take is on dangerous ground. In his fine book about lake flies, Commander C. F. Walker says he has never found an alder inside a trout. I'll bet he's never found $\frac{1}{4}$lb of cooked broad beans inside one, either. But I have. I have also found such other unusual dainties as a dead rat, a tin-opener (minus handle), and a number of fried, chip-potatoes.

This might give some support to the argument that, given correct presentation, even a tin-opener will serve to catch a trout. What the advocates of such notions conveniently overlook, however, is that trout may also be found to contain large numbers of one kind of organism, usually an insect. It is also possible to find in a trout's stomach one or more layers, each composed of a mass of insects or other organisms of the same kind and in the same state. Moreover, it is much more common to find this sort of thing inside a trout than it is to find tin-openers.

Of course, it is also not uncommon to find a mixture of all sorts of different organisms inside a trout. But surely everyone must accept, willingly or otherwise, that selective feeding by trout is quite common; that some trout sometimes feed on a particular food organism to the exclusion of all others, even when others are available. I would be inclined to think that an angler who refused to accept this must be one whose experience and knowledge of trout is limited.

It seems reasonable to assume that the ratio of selective to non-selective feeders is variable. It is likely to vary from one water to another, and from day to day, even from hour to hour, on any one water.

Commander Walker quotes K. R. Allen as stating that of 180 trout of which the stomach contents had been examined, 65 per cent had selected one food-animal and a further 6 per cent two food-animals. This means that in the water concerned, an artificial fly that failed to appear to the selective trout as one of the food-animals they were eating would not have been taken by any of those trout.

One does not need to examine the odds against any artificial fly selected at random happening to be an imitation of the food-animal selected by the trout to see that there must be at least some advantage in designing, tying and choosing the right artificial to imitate what the trout, or what some of the trout, are selecting at any given time and place.

The validity of that proposition is undisturbed, except in degree, by variations in the ratio of selective to unselective trout in different waters. If one trout in the water you are fishing is selective and no others, you will not catch that one trout unless you offer it a plausible imitation of what it is selecting. By so much will your opportunity to catch trout be reduced. It is necessary to add that this does not mean that effective imitation renders efficient presentation unnecessary.

There are two aspects of presentation. One consists of putting the artificial fly where the trout can see it in a manner that avoids alarming the fish. This is largely a matter of casting. The other aspect lies in influencing the behaviour of the fly after it has been cast. This influence may vary from studiously avoiding any movement of the fly other than what would be given to the natural insect by current and by wind, to the calculated attempt to impart movement in imitation of the real insect's voluntary movements. Particular cases include the avoidance of drag in dry-fly fishing on a river, and the retrieve of a sunken nymph by a series of pulls or twitches in lake or reservoir fishing.

It can therefore be said that at least part of presentation is part of imitation, but we cannot stop there, because there is more meaning in this statement than may at first be apparent. If we can agree that at least some trout are selective, then we must consider by what means their selection is carried out.

It must surely be by visual observation of a number of factors or features; that is, by more than one factor. If only one factor were involved, the selection by trout as we know it to take place would be impossible. Their stomachs would be found to contain food-animals that were uniform only in a particular respect and variable in others. They might be all of the same colour, but highly variable in shape and size; or uniform in size, but variable in shape and colour.

In fact, we find in the stomachs of trout that have been feeding selectively a high degree of uniformity in the food-animals eaten. This must surely support the view that the factors or features by which trout recognise particular food-animals are multiple. They may include size, shape, colour, texture, distribution of both colour and physical features, translucency, movement, and other features.

Experience in the design and use of artificial flies leads us to suppose that the inclusion of all the features by which a trout is capable of selecting a particular sort of food-animal is unnecessary. Indeed, it can fairly be argued that it is not only unnecessary, but impossible. At this stage readers will no doubt recall how many times they have heard or seen it stated that 'exact imitation is impossible, anyway!' Well, of course, exact imitation is impossible, and we need no diatribes about how wrong F. N. Halford was in attempting it.

Every would-be pundit on fly-fishing likes to have a cock-shy at Aunt Sally Halford, but few realise that his relative failure as a designer of artificial flies was not in what he attempted but in what he achieved. I use the word 'relative' because some of Halford's dressings are very effective, but many more are not. Those that are not fail because they are insufficiently good imitations in the eyes of the trout, not because they imitate the natural too well.

Halford's flies in no way invalidate the perfectly sound idea that if you want to catch a trout that is selecting only a particular species of insect, you must present it with an artificial fly that to the trout sufficiently resembles that species of insect. If you don't, you won't catch it.

I might have said that you must present this trout with an artificial that it cannot distinguish from the species it is selecting. I did not because to do so would be incorrect. An artificial may deceive a trout if it is looking for points of resemblance, but will fail to do so if it is looking for points of difference. Which it does depends on its experience.

In the case of a trout that lacks experience of artificial flies, what is needed is an artificial in the appearance and behaviour of which are combined enough points of similarity to trigger off the trout's brain, or central nervous system—call it what you will—and thus cause the fish to take your fly. It is part of the art of the designer and tyer of artificial flies to examine the real insect and divine which of its visual features he must include in his artificial and how he may best do this with the materials at his disposal, with some regard to the method of presentation to be used, because he wants to imitate behaviour as well as appearance if he can.

This is not, however, the whole art of a fly-designer. There are two conditions in which a selectively-feeding trout may be found where this alone is not enough. A trout may have been pricked or hooked and lost on an artificial fly that contained enough points of recognition to deceive it. If the artificial also contained enough dissimilar points, it will probably fail to deceive the trout again. A similar combination of discrepancies may trigger off not the desire to eat, but fear and flight. Fear always overrides all but the most extreme hunger in animals.

With such a trout, the fly-tyer must preserve such points of resemblance as will serve to attract, but eliminate or substitute such features as may, in combination, alarm the fish.

The other condition in which different factors may have to be considered is in a glut of food-animals, when they are so numerous that a trout cannot eat all that are available.

If a fish is eating only one in 50 of the natural flies that pass over or by it, then the angler using a most perfect imitation of the natural may fail to tempt the trout. Indeed, the fewer the points of difference, the longer may be the odds against the artificial being accepted.

Experience has led me to believe that in such cases the introduction of a single startling point of difference may induce the trout to select the artificial fly from among a large number of available natural insects.

It is certain that in many cases when large trout have been eating some of many mayflies, an artificial that included a few turns of hot-orange cock-hackle in its dressing was accepted at the first offer, after other artificial mayflies that had proved most effective in sparser hatches had been refused. I cannot deny, however, that in this there must remain an element of speculation.

Logically, then, it must be clear that, with certain provisos, there is much to be gained and nothing to be lost by devising artificial flies that include, from the trout's point of view, as many points of resemblance to the natural fly that the trout is selecting as possible. If, in fact, we strive for exact imitation in the true sense of the term, we shall catch more trout, and, I venture to add, enjoy catching them more.

It remains only to speculate why this point of view is so often bitterly opposed. Is it that some anglers would rather see it proved that any old artificial will serve, because they would like to avoid the complication involved in finding out what trout are eating and then finding a suitable artificial? Or is it that they resent the inference which protagonists of exact imitation have made in the past that the use of an artificial in which no attempt is made to imitate anything is unethical?

I hasten to say that I infer nothing of the sort. If an angler would rather sally forth with a collection of folk-lore instead of artificials that strive to resemble real insects, that is his business, though he ought to realise that his catches will be lighter to a greater or lesser extent, and that such of his *objets d'art* as succeed do so because some trout thought they were some kind of food-animal. The angler may neither know nor care which, though the trout, if they could talk, would be able to tell him. A trout does not take a fly in mistake for a jet aircraft or a house-brick.

In the case of many of the fancifully named products of Scotland, Ireland, Somerset and even Northamptonshire, not only the trout but many an experienced angler may be able to decide what an artificial imitates with more certainty and accuracy than its inventor.

If you snip the wings off your standard lake-flies, you may see more readily what I mean, and at the same time eliminate from many of these patterns, points of difference while retaining points of resemblance.

May 1967   *Richard Walker*

Silverhorns on the lake

Among the commonest of the smaller sedge-flies found on lakes and reservoirs are the various kinds of silverhorn. These are slender flies when seen resting on a grass stem or leaf and, when measured from the tip of the folded wings to the head, vary in length according to species, from about $\frac{1}{4}$in to $\frac{3}{4}$in. The antennae or horns are very thin and are usually more than twice, and sometimes three times, as long as the flies themselves. From their slim build and long horns the flies can be distinguished from all other sedge-flies, and even when they are flying the long horns can often be seen.

On some types the horns are a bright silvery-white with faint blackish annulations and the wings are black. This kind is, as it were, the prototype, as a specimen is illustrated in Ronalds's *Fly-fisher's Entomology* and is called by him the 'silver horns'. Francis Francis was more specific as he called this fly the 'black silver horns' and mentioned that another type, the 'brown silver horns', was taken freely by trout on the Itchen. One of the brown silverhorns has speckled brownish wings which in pattern and colour resemble some

24

Rutland Water—certainly the biggest (until Keilder opens) and possibly the best trout reservoir in the country

of the paler brown mottled feathers on a grouse, and this particular fly has for many years been called the grouse wing.

These three flies, the grouse wing, the black silverhorn and the brown silverhorn, are of considerable importance during the summer months. They are mainly evening flies and the best rises of fish to them occur after sunset. Many times in July and August the only steady rise of fish I have seen all day has been during a warm evening, when large numbers of these small sedge-flies have come on to the water.

As happens with other flies, different conditions in lakes and reservoirs suit different species of silverhorn. For instance, in the foothills of the Dublin mountains there is a small reservoir where the grouse wing is found in big swarms, but other kinds of silverhorn are scarce or absent. Here, on nearly any suitable afternoon in July, August or early September small swarms of these flies may be seen hovering over the grassy verges of the reservoir. As the afternoon advances the swarms increase in size. Towards sunset the swarms merge into each other and on particularly suitable evenings will form a continuous layer of flies hovering along the shore-line on the sheltered side of the reservoir.

The first time I fished this reservoir was with a friend who told me that there was a good rise of trout each evening, but that they were extremely difficult to catch. At that time I knew very little about silverhorns and had never knowingly fished for trout which were rising to them. By chance, I tied on a small Grey Sedge dry fly dressed to imitate the grey flag, which in those days hatched pro-fusely on some of the local rivers. To my friend's surprise, and most certainly to my own, nearly every trout which I covered rose to it.

I went home also with the erroneous idea that my friend had exaggerated the difficulty in catching those fish, and that they would rise to any small sedge-fly. In this I was soon disillusioned, as on my next visit there I did not catch any fish and cannot remember rising one.

The following day I tied some more Grey Sedges. (WING: Wood-cock. BODY: Grey seal's fur with gold wire rib. RIBBING AND FRONT HACKLES: Rusty dun cock. HOOK: Number 1.) I also dressed a few on which speckled partridge-tail fibres were substituted for the wood-cock feather in the wing.

On subsequent visits to the reservoir I was relieved to find that the fish took both these patterns, but as they seemed to show a slight preference for the pattern tied with the partridge-tail feather, I adopted that dressing for future use.

When a pattern is tied on a number o or a number 1 hook and dressed with short-fibred hackles with the wings lying close along the

A bank fisherman wading off the end of the Hambleton Peninsula at Rutland Water

body of the fly and projecting beyond the bend of the hook, I find it gives consistently good results when used at the appropriate time. But if the fish are not feeding on the natural flies which it represents, then it is liable to be ignored.

I had an interesting example of this selectiveness of fish one windy afternoon on Lough Sheelin when there was a considerable assortment of silverhorns of various shades and other small sedge-flies lying on the water in a fairly extensive calm area in the lee of a wooded point. Lough Sheelin is extremely rich in fly-life; and over a period of only a few years, by making casual collections of sedge-flies, I have found 31 species there, not counting the minute-sized sedges which seemingly are of no value for angling purposes. Some of the species, as might be expected, were rare, some were found in moderate numbers, and others were extremely common. A few species such as one of the black silverhorns, *Mystacides azurea*, appears on the lake in tremendous swarms. The grouse wing, *M. longicornis*, which predominates on the reservoir already mentioned, occurs on Sheelin only in comparatively moderate numbers.

On the particular afternoon I noticed that numerous black silverhorns were on the water, and I thought I saw some of them taken by the fish. Unfortunately, I had no small dark-coloured sedges with me, so I tried an Alder and then a Red Sedge which were on fairly large hooks, but these also were refused. Finally, as I had some fly-tying material in my bag, I dressed a dark type of sedge with a wing of rook, body of rook-herl and two small furnace cock-hackles on a number 1 hook. The change in the behaviour of the fish was immediate when they saw this fly. I caught two of them, rose and missed two others, and lost the fifth and seemingly largest, which jumped as soon as I tightened on him.

The third type of silverhorn, the brown silverhorn of Francis Francis, has wings of various shades of greyish-brown with a rather dark body and legs. These silverhorns in company with the grouse wing appear in tremendous numbers on some lakes. During the past season they came out in clouds on Lough Glore in Co Westmeath in July and August, and many trout, some of more than 4lb which rose in the late evening to feed on them, were caught by dry-fly anglers.

A pattern which was taken well there was dressed as follows: BODY: Dark-brown floss-silk with fine gold wire run up through a ribbing hackle of short-fibred red game-cock. WING: Thin strips of speckled grouse tied to lie close along the hook, and another small red game-cock hackle wound in front of the wing. HOOK: Number 0, 1 or 2.

To take full advantage of the rise of fish to silverhorns it is important to know something of the habits of these flies. One of the commonest and most widely-distributed of them in Britain and Ireland is the black silverhorn, *Mystacides azurea*. This is one of two species in the genus *Mystacides* and of several species in the genus *Leptocerus*, which together are grouped as black silverhorns. The following notes refer specifically to *M. azurea*, but they apply in general to the other common silverhorns.

Spring on the Usk, a river famed for its early season trout-fishing and hatches of March browns

Most lake anglers probably have often seen these flies hovering in swarms along the edge of the shore and over the shallows on the calm side of a lake. They fly within a foot or so of the ground or the water surface and their characteristic flight is quick and jerky; individual flies follow a course which consists of a series of small circles with the planes of the circles as it were vertical to the water, but as the circles do not quite overlap the line of flight follows a sort of corkscrew pattern. As the afternoon or evening advances, and the number of flies increases, the swarms extend further out over the water, perhaps for 40 or 50yd, and to anyone waiting for a rise of fish to begin the conditions look good. Then, for no apparent reason, the swarms may move back to the shore and the flies may disappear as they take shelter among the herbage. Shortly afterwards they may reappear and start their gyrations once more only again, after an interval, to return to shore.

This behaviour is due to small changes in the weather. These black silverhorns dislike flying in the direct rays of the sun, and they dislike low temperatures and wind. Consequently, the conditions which suit them best are dull, warm, muggy days, with little or no wind and the sun completely obscured by cloud. If, when they are swarming, the sun comes from behind cloud or a cold breeze springs up, the flies will make for shelter, and unless they find a place sheltered from both sun and wind, they resettle on adjacent vegetation until conditions change again to suit them.

These swarms consist of the male flies, and from time to time females join them. After mating the females fly back to the bushes and in fact, while still paired, the two flies will often be seen flying back together.

The female silverhorns remain hidden, usually until after sunset when the light has faded. Then, provided the air has remained warm enough, and the wind is not too strong, they move out over the lake on their ovipositing flight. When egg-laying is finished they fall, spent, on the water and their numbers augment the numbers of males which will have gradually dropped from the swarms which, on suitable evenings, will have been hovering over the water for several hours. Trout may start feeding on the male flies, but the main rise usually does not begin until the females appear.

Keeping these habits of the flies in mind, it can be seen that in bright calm weather there is an advantage in fishing from the west shore of an area of water, provided there are high trees on a hill along that shore behind which the sun drops an hour or two before it actually sets. If there is a wind, it should, of course, be westerly, so that there will be a sheltered area of calm water stretching out for some distance from the shore. Under such conditions the male silverhorns can be expected to hover over the calm water when flies on other parts of the lake which are not shaded from the sun, and which may be too exposed to the wind, will not take wing.

These black silverhorns are reluctant to fly at air temperatures below about 55°F and although small numbers of them may be seen hovering at some degrees lower than this, big swarms need not be expected. As with many other flies, trout are likely to ignore silverhorns unless plenty of them are on the water, so it is no use to expect a rise of fish to these flies on an evening which turns too chilly.

On lakes where the green or speckled peters, *Phryganea varia*, occur, these huge sedge-flies, in their season, start hatching at about the same time in the dusk as trout begin rising to silverhorns. Owing to the size of the peters—some of them have a wing span of 2in—and to the disturbances they make when scuttling along the surface towards the shore, they are very conspicuous and, not unnaturally, a trout feeding on silverhorns will seldom let one of these large mouthfuls go past. It is a great comfort then to mount an artificial peter, as not only is it a lot easier to hook and play a heavy trout on a fly tied on a number 6 or 7 hook with an appropriately heavy cast, than it is with a number 1 hook and a light cast, but the larger fly is much easier to see in the fading light.

Even so, if only a few peters are seen on the water it is worthwhile using one; by doing this I have taken trout which had plenty of silverhorns, but none of the larger sedge-flies in their stomachs. More frequently one or two peters will be found to be mixed up with a mass of silverhorns on autopsy. When there is a strong hatch of peters it hardly seems worthwhile using a silverhorn. Similarly, on lakes such as Lough Ennel, where big swarms of large chironomids or buzzers appear on the water at dusk, trout usually feed on them instead of on silverhorns. Occasionally I have found silverhorns in Lough Ennel trout, but the main food items of fish caught there on summer evenings are the pupal and adult peters and buzzers.

July 1961   *J. R. Harris*

March days on the Usk

I began my season last year with a week on the Usk in March and have been summing up the main impressions and lessons learnt during that stay. Fishing was possible on only four days out of the seven. If you plan to fish mountain-bred rivers like this one, you do well to have an alternative programme for days when rain brings them down in spate and makes fly-fishing impossible, unless, like me, you are content to be by the river and delight in exploring its banks.

The large olive is the backbone of spring fly-fishing on most early rivers, and the Usk is no exception. There was a fair sprinkling on the water on the first day of my visit, March 24, and Lionel Sweet told me later that they were the first he'd seen on the river that year.

The Usk is also a river where the March brown occurs, more especially in April. I saw it only on the last afternoon of my stay, when those hatching were all very dark males. This big dun is remarkably variable in general coloration and Mrs Sweet dresses the artificial in several appropriate body shades, mottling the stiff floating hackle to realistic effect with a touch of partridge.

The true March brown is very much a locally-distributed dun. Even Usk March browns are not always what they seem. On Wing-Commander Haworth-Booth's length of the Gwyrne, a small tributary which joins the Usk near Cwrt-y-Gollen, I saw March brown-like duns which on closer examination proved to be large brook duns (*Ecdyonurus torrentis*). This fly also occurs on the main river, and I was shown specimens taken there by Dr Michael Wade, of Risca, who preserves natural duns and spinners in attractive, polished, labelled blocks of synthetic resin.

As expected I saw quite a few early brown stoneflies, to which the reaction of trout is somewhat unpredictable. I had dressed a few artificial Early Browns and March Browns to take with me, besides a good stock of Imperials. The latter pattern, imitating the male large olive dun, is unbeatable for catching early spring trout, anywhere. It is worth mentioning, in this connection, that of scores of large olives I caught and examined each day, all were males.

The downstream cast is particularly valuable in Usk dry-fly fishing. On one of my best days most of my trout were taken in this way. On that occasion there was only one place where I could gain access to the water below a vertical high bank, and most of the feeding trout on the whole beat were rising in a concentration in a little bay some way downstream from my position. Such chalk-stream refinements as the overland cast are quite useless when the drop from bank-lip to water surface is 20ft or more!

High water prevented wading during my visit. The banks are sometimes so high and thickly wooded that putting a fly on the surface is not easy, and back-casting is virtually impossible. Roll-casting is always a useful asset to the fly-fisher, but on the Usk it is indispensable.

Each morning, going out to fish water I had never seen before, preliminary reconnaissance and careful appreciation were necessary to determine where trout were most likely to be found rising once large olives began to come up. In the high-water conditions prevailing, rising fish were sometimes confined to a length of only 15 to 20yd on reaches a mile or more in extent. Unless one was in the right place at the right time, little sport could be expected. But if the appreciation was accurate, one could take trout after trout on the dry fly from about noon onwards, and go on doing so for several hours, although it was still only March in a backward season.

The main factors to be taken into account are applicable to most early fly-rivers. These are the type of water from which large olives can be expected to hatch, the set of the wind to string them under the bank within fishing reach, likely hides for trout in these localities, the set of the adjacent currents past these hides, and the most likely dun-productive lies which trout occupy when on the feed.

The practical fly-fisher's main concern with entomology is to teach himself the solution of simple problems of this nature. These factors vary in importance from river to river, but after the first day or two on a strange water it is easier to gauge their relative local significance. On the Usk, for example, feeding lies varied from day to day, and sometimes during the day, the principal element responsible being wind. This was my main ally.

The Usk produces plenty of duns—large olives were on the water throughout most days of my stay—but fish tended to ignore scattered duns hatching in midstream and the thing to do was to join the trout at the receiving end of dun concentrations. A shift in the fickle wind sometimes necessitated returning to the car, driving to the nearest bridge, perhaps some miles away, and then on to another fishing position on the opposite bank. In cases like this, involving loss of time, you have to back your own judgment, which is part of the risk and charm of spring trouting.

I never found the Usk dull, even on the days when high, discoloured water made fishing impossible. I was sheltering one afternoon as wind-driven sleet lashed the bare black oaks beneath the slopes of Dan-y-Warren. The storm passed and suddenly the sun came out and light and shadows raced and played across the tinted hills.

A rainbow formed, its near end dipping into the Gwyrne inflow opposite where I crouched, and through it, as if to gild the lily, a kingfisher flew. Larks sang overhead. Flurries of large olives whirled across the drift of snowdrops blooming at my feet, but no trout moved this day. No matter, I caught a great many during my short visit and most of them went back to fight again.

March 1964   *Oliver Kite*

The art of winging flies

Of all the questions I am asked when I give a fly-tying demonstration, three out of four will be about putting wings on trout flies, for most home fly-tyers find this difficult because the processes are hidden by the fingers. Donald Downs has the unique combination of artistic and fly-tying ability, and he helps me here to explain what is

34

happening as well as how to do the job properly. Let us take a simple wet-fly first.

It is important to start with a stout feather and go on to softer plumages, such as barred teal and mallard, later. The grey mallard primaries are excellent to work with if you make sure that they are fresh and not dried out with age. Old feathers split easily.

Fig 1 shows two wing-slips removed from opposing primaries, a left- and a right-hand wing feather. These slips could be cut, but I prefer to tear them from the quill, because the quill adhering to the roots helps to keep the fibres together. If you strip the base fibres from the feathers, you can work evenly along each quill. The wing-slips should be of equal width and shade of colour.

Fig 2 shows the wing-slips matched against each other, tip to tip. In England we normally have the wet-fly wings curving into each

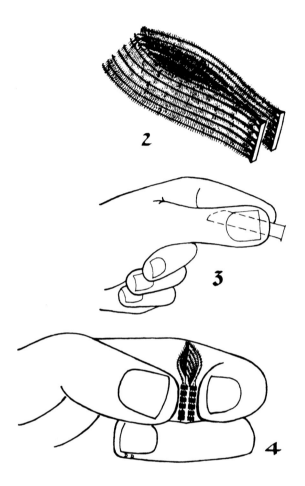

other to make a flat wing, but this isn't universal, and many Irish
and Welsh types prefer the wings to be matched back to back, as in
a dry fly, to give them a flair in the water.

Fig 3 shows the wing-slips grasped between the finger and thumb
of the left hand, ready for tying. In Fig 4 we have an imaginary view
of the slips matched against each other, front to front, with the dull
side of the feather facing outwards.

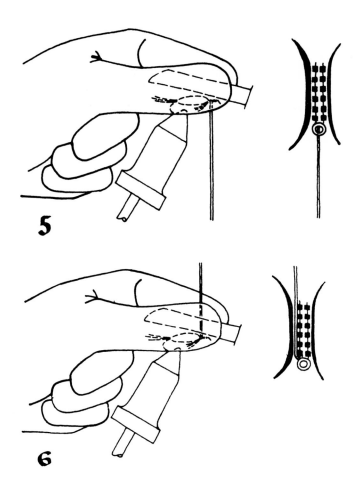

5

6

The wing-slips are held on top of the hook-shank in the left hand so that there is no gap between the lower fibres and the shank. A layer of tying silk has formed a bed for the wings and the silk returns to a place immediately in front of the body. The front view shows the perfect position (Fig 5).

Now the silk is raised as in Fig 6 and pinched tight. Again, the front view shows what is happening. The thread is taken over the

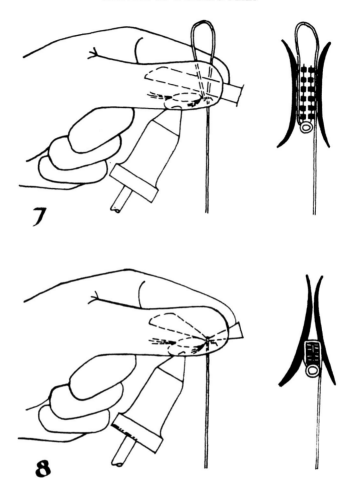

wings and pinched again on the far side so that the slips are now held between the fingers in a loose loop of silk. This is very important. Fig 7 shows exactly how this must be.

In Fig 8 the thread is pulled tight from below, and we see the reason for the loose loop, for were it made tight as it was being formed it would twist the wings round the hook-shank. The direction of pull from below should compress each fibre on top of its fellows like a concertina. This is the secret of winging. Once the first loop has been pulled tight, two or three more loops can be made in the same way before releasing the wings.

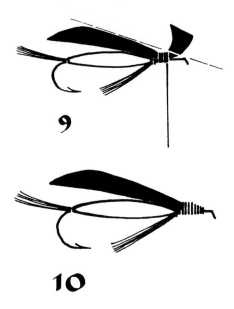

In Fig 9 we see the finishing of the head. The roots of the wings are raised and trimmed away by scissors laid flat along the hook-shank. This gives the roots a nice taper for covering with silk to make a neat head. It is important to work to the right with the silk, for if you cover your first turns again you will flatten your wings, or split them. The set of the wings is governed by the first loop of silk you pull tightly (Fig 8). Finally, finish off with a whip knot, trim away the tail of the thread, and give the head a couple of coats of clear cellulose varnish, not forgetting to clear the eye of varnish. If all goes well you will have a shape like that shown in Fig 10, the perfect fly.

Now for some further pointers. The hackle is put in before the wing, and is shown in Fig 5. The normal way is to wind in the hackle in front of the body, divide it equally on top of the hook-shank, and pull the fibres below into the wet-fly position, keeping them there with diagonal turns of thread. However, this can make an ugly hump on top of the hook which cocks the wing upwards.

Many anglers prefer a low, slim wing, and this can be achieved by tying in a bunch of hackle fibres under the hook-shank. This is a 'false hackle' and it is tied in like the wings on the underside of the hook. The hook can be turned upside down in the vice for this if you find it easier. It is important to tie in the hackle immediately in front of the body, whichever way you do it, so that the wings sit on top of the hackle, which results in a neat head.

When you are proficient with strong feathers, you may proceed to the softer teal and mallard. You can take slips from alternate right and left flank feathers, but one dodge which results in a stronger wing is to tear out a wide strip from a single feather and roll it up like a carpet to give three layers of fibre. Before tying-in, it should be moistened and slicked into a neat wing shape.

You can buy special tweezers to hold the slips for winging, but nothing can beat the natural feel of the fingers, which develops with practice.

You may think that I am fussy over tiny details, but they are all essential to get a perfect fly. One of my favourite writers, 'Lemon Grey', related how a lopsided wing could make a fly skew in the water. I share his view that wings are important to a fly and that they must be tied on correctly.

July 1968   *Geoffrey Bucknall*

Observations on chironomids

Over the years much has been written about the aquatic life on which river-fish feed. On the other hand, apart from one or two books published comparatively recently, little reading is available on the aquatic organisms that inhabit lakes and reservoirs.

Most still-waters contain a greater variety of aquatic creatures than rivers. The subject is therefore more complex and the lack of angling literature adds to the difficulties facing the student observer. During the past three seasons, in conjunction with that well-known angler and entomologist, David Jacques, I have made some interesting observations, and as a result of raising various insects in tanks under controlled conditions, combined with observations in the field, we have made many enlightening discoveries.

As far as possible we have confined our observations to the same species or family, but in the course of this past year I went off at a slight tangent and started a personal study of the *Chironomidae*.

I find these insects quite fascinating and without a doubt they are responsible for a large proportion of the still-water trout's diet, particularly in their pupal stages. However, before I go further, I must make it clear that my study of the family, which comprises nearly 400 species, has been restricted to a few particular types.

Chironomid species vary in size from adults with a wing length of less than 1mm to those with a wing length of nearly 8mm. Both the pupae and adult winged flies also vary considerably in colour, with bodies ranging from orange to brown, green or black. Therefore, for simplicity's sake from the fly-fisherman's point of view, they can be classified by the aforementioned colours and by their sizes, which may be described as small, medium and large.

The chironomids, or buzzers or midges as some anglers prefer to call them, are part of the extremely large *Diptera* order. The females have fairly stout cylindrical bodies, while the males are slimmer. Both have two semi-transparent wings, usually shorter than their bodies. Many species hatch in vast numbers early in the morning or late evening, others at any hour of the day.

Little is known about their life-cycle, but personal observation of certain species has revealed that the adult females lay their eggs on the surface in clusters in the form of beads. The small larvae which eventually emerge swim to the bed of the lake where they remain for a considerable period, living either in small tunnels in the mud or forming cases of such things as decayed vegetable matter and silt.

These vary in size according to species, the largest I have seen being nearly an inch long. During this period some species are found browsing or moving with a characteristic figure-of-eight lashing movement along the bed of the lake or immobile in weed, particularly blanket weed.

The colour of these larvae varies from a pale brown or green through to a brilliant red and it is thought that this latter colour is due to haemoglobin in the blood. This substance has the property of absorbing oxygen and distributing it through the body of the larva. In well-oxygenated water many specimens which in their larval stages are often a dull brown-red colour become a brilliant red shortly before pupation.

It is fairly easy to tie a lifelike representation of these larvae by using a size 12 or 14 fine-wire, long-shank hook and merely tying a body of red or green marabou silk mixed with a judicious amount of fluorescent floss of the same colour and ribbed with a fine silver wire. Unfortunately, it is a difficult pattern to fish, owing to the virtual impossibility of representing the laboured movements of the larvae along the mud-bottom. However, I have had a certain amount of success by retrieving such artificials exceedingly slowly along the bottom.

The pupation period of the chironomids I have observed has been between 12 and 24 hours. In its final stage the pupa ascends into the surface film where it remains hanging in a vertical position with the filaments on top of its head breaking the surface. It remains in this position for anything up to an hour, wriggling at constant intervals.

At rest the pupae have a strongly-curved body with a slightly bulbous thorax. The top of the thorax is covered with fine white filaments which no doubt assist respiration, and the tails of most specimens I have handled have small appendages, usually of a distinct whitish colour. As transformation to the adult approaches, the movement of the pupa gradually decreases until it ceases completely. The pupa, now as stiff as a poker, slowly swings upwards and assumes a horizontal position in the film. Within seconds the skin of the pupal case splits along the thorax and the adult winged fly emerges on the surface.

It is during this final stage of pupation when the pupae are hanging in the film that the trout feed on them avidly with the familiar slow head-and-tail rise. As most anglers know, it is when a widespread rise of this nature is in progress that the fish are often most difficult to catch. I am, therefore, of the opinion that it is most important to observe the following points if one wants to increase one's chances of success.

The artificial must be a reasonably accurate representation of the pupa. The size and colour of the natural on the water at the time should be simulated. The artificial should be fished either without movement or exceedingly slowly in small jerks, and it must be fished in the surface film.

Since adopting the above points my catches have increased considerably, and for those of my readers who are interested, the dressings that I have developed to represent these midge pupae are given below.

Hatching pupa. HOOK: Down-eyed wide-gape fine-wire 12 to 16. SILK: As body colour. TAG: White flure floss. Tie a sparse bunch well round bend on hook. BODY: Black, brown, orange or green marabou silk, ribbed sparsely with narrow silver 'Lurex' and then covered with opaque PVC. THORAX: Green or purple peacock-herl. FILAMENTS: The fine fluffy down from base of white hen-feather.

The body should be continued well round the bend of the hook to represent the strongly curved shape of the pupa, and the filaments should be tied through the thorax, but facing forward and upward over the eye of the hook.

I have had considerable success fishing this pattern in mid-water in tiny jerks during the day when no surface-feeding fish have been observed. It seems reasonable to suppose that these pupae do spend some time in mid-water, although I have so far been unable to substantiate this. I have, however, caught many trout during these periods that have been full of the pupae.

43

When fishing the artificial described in this manner, I use the pattern minus the rib of silver 'Lurex'. 'Lurex' is necessary only in the hatching pattern to represent the translucent appearance of the body of the pupa immediately before transition to the adult.

April 1968   *John Goddard*

A team of loch flies

In theory, the greater the number of fly patterns carried, the better is the chance of being able to produce the right fly at the right time. In practice, it does not work out that way. The more patterns carried, the greater is the chance of choosing the wrong one, and an over-full fly-box leads to thinking that it is the fly which is wrong when the fish are not taking, whereas, nine times out of ten, it is the presentation of the fly which is wrong. A change of method is generally better than a change of fly, and little good comes from changing fly after fly.

Wet flies are not imitations of natural creatures. They convey an impression of small fry, shrimps, nymphs or pupae according to the way in which they are fished, and method of fishing must therefore be more important than pattern.

Size of fly is also more important than pattern, and it is generally better to try a change of size before deciding to change the pattern. For this reason one pattern in two sizes is better than two patterns in one size.

The business of limiting the contents of a fly-box is complicated not only by the vast number of patterns available, but by variations in the dressings of many standard patterns. These variations are attempts to improve upon a pattern which has been proved to be good, and such variations mostly depend upon suiting, or adapting, an original dressing to existing conditions of light. This idea is a good one and increases the interest of fishing, but it should not be allowed to overcrowd the fly-box.

The flies actually to be fished are best chosen at the water-side, with due consideration to water, light, and what can be seen of the

44

Trout and Salmon writer, Bruce Sandison, fishes lonely Loch Leir, close to the Sutherland–Caithness border

trout. The team from which the flies are selected is best made on 'form' at home, and 'form' is past performance judged from records and experience.

My own list of flies varies from year to year to about the same extent as does the list of children's Christian names published each year in *The Times*. Recently the Zulu has come into favour, whereas I seldom used to fish it, while the Black Pennell, which was always a favourite, now hardly gets a place. The general weather pattern of recent seasons may be a cause, or it may be just rheumatism. On the other hand, some patterns are never far from the top of my list: Hardy's Favourite, Claret and Mallard, Greenwell, and March Brown.

With these thoughts in mind I have selected some of the casts which have done best on Highland lochs during the past few seasons. In each case they are given in the order tail–dropper–bob.

APRIL
> Bright day: Zulu–March Brown–Red Palmer.
> Dull day: Blae and Black–Claret and Mallard–Black Spider.

MAY
> As for April, but add Invicta–Greenwell–March Brown.

JUNE AND JULY
> Bright day: Teal and Green–Greenwell–Butcher.
> Dull day: Grouse and Green–Woodcock and Hare's Ear–Woodcock and Yellow.

AUGUST
> Bright day: Zulu–Peter Ross–Red Palmer.
> Dull day: Grouse and Claret–Teal and Red–Black Spider.

SEPTEMBER
> Bright day: Greenwell–Dunkeld–Butcher.
> Dull day: Invicta–Grouse and Claret–Worm Fly.

I now have: Hardy's Favourite, Claret and Mallard, Greenwell, March Brown, Zulu, Red Palmer, Blae and Black, Black Spider, Invicta, Teal and Green, Grouse and Green, Butcher, Woodcock

46

From Leir's neighbour, Loch Sletill, a glorious pre-lunch bag of wild brown trout

and Yellow, Woodcock and Hare's Ear, Peter Ross, Teal and Red, Grouse and Claret, Dunkeld, and the Worm Fly.

That makes 19 patterns for the whole season, but I would not carry them all for the whole season. Until the end of May the probables are mostly blacks and reds. Then come the greens, olives and yellows in June and July. The blacks and reds come back again in August. The reds remain during September when they are joined by olives and yellows. It is impossible to forecast just how the season will work out, but it is not very difficult to limit the team to a dozen probables at any one time. And there is much to be gained by doing so.

May 1962   *H. A. Oatts*

47

Confidence in flies

I once bought a deadly trout fly. It caught fish after fish until its original dressing was almost unrecognisable. Then it caught an over-hanging branch of a tall tree! No other example of the same pattern seemed to approach its effectiveness. There was something about that fly I have never been able to fathom or to copy.

I am also reminded of a certain Olive Nymph that once had a magnetic effect on the trout on a stream in Wiltshire. I kept the actual fly for a long time and on many occasions copied its most obvious features, but never succeeded in reproducing the killing qualities of the original. Many, I am sure, will recognise this enigma. What is there to be said about it?

There is one likely comment: 'It is all a matter of confidence'.

After a fly has been successful on a number of occasions, it is fished with an added degree of confidence which contributes towards further success. Confidence in a pattern, or a particular example of a pattern, is certainly a telling factor and not to be lightly dismissed.

Personally, I have little reason to put any great faith in a dry Greenwell's Glory, yet I am sure it is every bit as good an imitation of an olive dun as the pattern I prefer, and, wielded by a more confident rod, would deceive just as many trout.

Confidence largely comes as something built up through successful past experiences. An angler learns to say 'yes' in his mind to a particular example even before he has presented it to a single fish. Maybe to him it looks right, and so he makes his selection from half-a-dozen artificials which on casual observation are identical.

It comes in time—this ability to assess which one to choose. And perhaps one of the best ways of acquiring such perception is to tie one's own flies, to observe the precise dressing of successful patterns, and the characteristics of individual artificials that outfish the rest. Thus, what must often appear to the beginner to be remarkable intuition, may, after all, be born largely of experience.

I doubt whether it is possible to tie a few flies which are in every respect identical. Hook shapes and sizes are supposed to be standardised, but anyone with average eyesight knows that in any dozen hooks of a given size and pattern there will be visible differences in the cut of the barbs. Even when two very similar hooks have been found, how is it possible to match exact quantities and qualities of covering materials from tail whisks to varnished head?

It may well be argued that a trout does not mind very much if your offering is ribbed with three turns of silver instead of four, if the body of one pattern is a fraction of an inch longer than that of another, and if the tying silk employed is black when the professionals say it should be dark brown.

Nevertheless, a combination of such differences can radically alter the appearance of the offering, and it is time well spent at least to search for the right quality and size of hackle, to rib the body with the most seemly thickness of tinsel, to set the wing at the correct rake and to ensure that its length is in proportion to the hook size and characteristic of the natural.

I readily grant that such attention to detail becomes ludicrous if the fly is then crashed on to the surface of the water by some extrovert attired in a garb of many colours to match his air of gay abandon.

Perhaps the ideal is to strike a happy balance and to guard against offering the trout some of the examples that are offered to the public, while, at the same time, also admitting the need of a total presentation of the fly which must, of necessity, be attached to the leader, line, reel and fisherman.

Below are listed four excellent patterns and one or two confidence-inspiring features I look for in their dressing.

THE COACHMAN: It may come in a variety of sizes, but fish it small if the surface is well rippled with a good breeze, or the trout may come short. The body of this fly should, for most waters in reasonable condition, be of bronze peacock-herl—a definite copper colour—and plump. The wing should lie in a flat half-moon close to this body and extend not much beyond the bend of the hook. The hackle (red–ginger) should have some sparkle and not be too short.

THE HAWTHORN FLY: I now use only one pattern which I fish wet on a size 3 round-bend hook (size 10, old number). The gently-tapered body must be black and shiny. This can be achieved by a coat of varnish over black tying-silk ribbed with fine copper or silver wire. A long, glassy, cock-hackle should rake over the body beyond the bend of the hook and be assisted to do so by a pronounced thorax of black ostrich-herl at the head of the fly.

THE SILVER MARCH BROWN: In this excellent sedge imitation I look for whisks of brown mallard-fibres, a body of hare's ear ribbed with wide, flat, silver tinsel, and a wing of paired pieces of hen pheasant, secondary feathers. The wing tips should be rounded—by burning with a cigarette end—to a blunt, jagged finish, and the dark partridge-hackle should be sparse and put on last.

WILLIAM'S FAVOURITE: Choose a small size (1–3) hook for trout and sea trout. Aim for a gently-tapered body of black, floss silk ribbed with only three turns of narrow, silver tinsel. Choose a fairly short, dense black, hen-hackle and give the wet fly a few fibres of it for whisks.

The angler who aims for precision in all aspects of presentation will be the one most likely to satisfy both himself and the trout.

May 1967   *Frederick Mold*

Dealing with dimplers

It occurs at other times, too, but most typically in the evenings of warm days. You come to a bend in the river or a backwater aside from the main stream and find the surface dimpled with tiny rings. Obviously, fish are feeding on something in the surface layers.

You may think them very small fish, but a few moments of observation will usually disabuse you of that notion. Often they are good trout, wasting none of their energy but intent on making a steady meal of whatever is on the water.

They put their lips to the surface and draw in small mouthfuls of water along with their food. This makes tiny hollows in the calm surface with hardly any other disturbance. The trout, for the most part, are gliding a few inches under, and at an angle to, the surface, sipping here and there.

Because you can see nothing on the water you may think of nymphs or hatching duns. Sometimes you succeed in getting a pluck at your representations of these, but you are unlikely to feel you have solved the mystery. If you persist in more than one or two casts, you only succeed in putting the trout down.

I never failed to be interested in this phenomenon and always had a go. Because it was a case of surface-feeding, I would try dry fly, hatching nymph, and nymph in that order, but never had much success.

Then one afternoon the river was in sudden flood after a morning of torrential rain and I had no success with bait and no hope of fly-fishing. I sat down beside a large eddy, where the current reversed itself, to drink a flask of tea and eat my bite. The eddy was fringed on the bank side with small items of flotsam and a collar of dirty foam. Between this and the strong main current the surface was quite smooth, circulating slowly.

The top two or three inches of the calm patch were almost clear, but lower down this transparency was lost in the thickening layers of silt-loaded water. Then I noticed the dimpling of the surface already described. I was on a high bank looking almost straight down. When I concentrated on the dimpled area I could see the trout coming up to the surface and sipping.

I hadn't yet seen their prey, but looking down into the debris on my side of the foam fringe I saw hundreds of tiny flies, floating on the surface with their wings flat out on either side of their dead bodies. In fact, it was not easy to see their wings at all. In clear water they would have been practically invisible by reason of their trans-parency.

The conclusion was instantaneous. The dimpling trout were taking spent spinners lying in the surface tension and rendered almost invisible because their transparent wings were not lifted up into the

51

A time for reflection rather than fishing. A trout-fisher on Ladybower Reservoir in Derbyshire finds an early season calm

air. Since they were dead or dying, the trout had no need of haste in taking them, hence the leisurely, sipping take.

Their very numbers encouraged exclusive feeding. Even if the trout noticed the angler's nymph or dry fly, the contrast of form and attitude of these would operate against their acceptance. Perhaps, therefore, now that the secret was out, a representation of an appropriate spent spinner would have a better chance of success.

I had no spent-spinner artificials with me. The best I could think of was to trim a hackled dry fly by cutting off all the fibres which fell below the hook-shank. This would allow the fly to lie in the surface film instead of above it.

I caught two fish out of that particular slack and added a few more by looking for similar eddies elsewhere on the stream. But I decided to be prepared for dimpling trout in the future.

Of course, you can buy hackle-point tyings designed for such occasions. If you make your own flies, these are quite simple variations on your usual methods. If you are not content with trimmed dry-flies, use iridescent cock-hackles such as will let the light shine through their fibres.

Tie them on with only the tips extending sideways from the shank. Badger, Blue Dun and Pale Olive are suitable varieties. Any Red Spinner recipe is likely to prove a suitable basis for a hackle-point fly. If a hackle is wound above the wings, as Halford recommended, use only a few turns, so as not to lift the fly out of the surface tension.

When 'Parachute' flies with horizontally-wound hackles were first invented, I learned to make my own. Nowadays I like to have a few in readiness for dimplers. I think they are better than hackle-points, which are rather fragile.

The 'dimpler-horizontal' is tied with only two, or at most three, turns of the hackle so as to preserve its transparency. The parachute effect ensures its flotation in the surface film, and the choice of body colour attends to the question of what type of fly.

This is how I make a horizontal fly. A piece of thin, soft wire (finest fuse wire is good) is tied at the shoulder of the shank by means of the body silk. Although my fly-vice is usually held in my hand, for this special purpose a bench-vice is better as it releases a hand to hold the wire taut and upright.

A hackle is tied in by its stump in the usual way, forward of the wire. Then, with the help of the hackle-pliers, it is wound the required number of turns round the base of the wire, not the hook-shank. After that it is fastened off below the wire and the unused portion snipped off.

Then the wire may be cut a fraction above the hackle and its tiny stub bent, or pressed down among the fibres. This works reasonably well and the hackle never seems to slip off the bent end. Alterna tively, the end can be bent down and tied in by the silk before the latter is fastened off. Finally, the body is varnished.

These 'dimpler-horizontals' are good when trout are behaving as I have described. They are also useful during the evening rise, which is often occasioned by a spinner fall at the end of a warm summer's day.

January 1966   *C. R. Pearce*

Black magic for blank days

The river was low and the trout were wary. For two days I had wooed them with everything I considered a self-respecting trout should want, but without so much as an offer. With four days of my week's holiday to go I repaired in deep despondency to the local tobacco, ice-cream and fishing-tackle dealer, and told him my troubles.

'You want,' he said, 'some blackish flies for the hill lochs, and on the river you want a Black Spider.'

'But what about the sea-trout?' I enquired.

'There's nothing they boys like half as much as a Black Spider,' he said.

And he was dead right of course, for I had the thrill of landing a brace of herling on the sea-pool that evening, and a sea-trout and a herling next day, all on the Black Spider.

After this I made up some casts of Blae and Black, Zulu and Black Spider and fished the hill lochs with them. The results were eminently satisfactory. I collected about a dozen three-quarter-pounders a day, with an occasional pounder for good measure.

However, I was much too happily engaged to risk losing good fishing time by trying a control experiment, so it may be argued that one might have done as well, or even better, with more colourful flies. But I am inclined to think not, for experience since then has consistently supported the 'black-hackle' theory. And black flies, particularly black-hackle flies, have been popular since the earliest records of fly-fishing.

Dame Juliana Berners (1486), mentions representations of the Hawthorn Fly. A couple of hundred years later Izaak Walton's collaborator, Charles Cotton, was recommending: 'A black body of the herl of an ostrich feather, rib'd with silver twist, and the black hackle of a cock over all.'

A couple of centuries after that W. C. Stewart, *The Practical Angler* (1857), was heading his list of artificial trout flies with his Black Spider: '[it is] made of the small feather of the cock starling, dressed with brown silk, and is, upon the whole, the most killing imitation we know.'

More recently Charles Kingsley in his *Chalk-stream Studies* eulogised the Alder: 'Toddling about in a black bonnet and a brown cloak.' And G. E. M. Skues once took eighteen brace of trout in one day, only two of them under a pound, on a Kingsley's Alder.

Indeed, many dark flies have stood the test of time; the Black Ant, Knotted Midge and so-called Black Gnat are indispensable at times, and among hardy perennials the Butcher, Black Palmer, Saltoun, and William's Favourite are great killers, while that doughty chironomid the Blae and Black is the mainstay and sheet anchor of most loch-fishers.

The large proportion of dark-coloured insects to be found in the stomachs of captured trout is a matter of frequent observation, and the angler needs no reminding that there are often more blackish-looking gnats, smuts and midges about the water—and his person—than there are duns or sedges.

The weight of all this evidence convinced me of the advantage of using a dark fly on the lochs whenever there was no definite indication to the contrary, a hatch of lake olives or green midges, for instance. But I was not so sure about the rivers until I struck a bad patch on the Aberdeenshire Don some years ago.

The conditions were excellent and every day there was a hatch of march browns. I tried the standard representations of the insect, male and female, but without success. I agreed wholeheartedly with Skues's observation that the artificial March Brown, 'is an excellent fly, and as generally tied quite a poor imitation of the natural fly, and quite a passable one of almost anything else'.

A Baigent's Brown was more productive, but although fish came to the fly, I found that I was hooking only about half of them. I attributed this to the smallness of the hook in relation to the length of the hackle, but retrospect suggests that it was probably due to faulty striking. A few fish fell to a Ginger Quill, but this fly was extremely difficult to see in the rough water at the heads of the pools, where most of the fish were rising. Dark Olives, Greenwell's Glories, Iron Blue Duns and Wickham's Fancies, being winged, were more easily seen, but the fish showed no enthusiasm for any of them.

Then I had the good fortune to meet an angler who had decided views of his own. He had fished that stretch of the river, on and off, for 30 years, and I gathered that originally his most successful fly had been a large Greenwell's Glory. Later he had taken to a Baigent's Brown, but for the last few years, he said, he had considered his own convenience rather than that of the trout and had evolved a fly which floated well and was easy to see.

He had three trout in his bag which between them must have weighed the better part of 6lb, and he had the kindness to present me with three of his flies. But although I noticed that he had one of them on his cast, I was none too sanguine, for the fly looked like nothing I had seen before. It had the shape and size of a mayfly, and it was just plain black.

It was more in gratitude than expectation that I put one on, oiled it and set off to look for a rising fish. As luck would have it, the only riser was an old enemy that had scorned my whole armamentarium for the last few days. I floated the black fly over him, and in less than 10 minutes that trout depressed the pointer of my spring balance to just beyond the 2lb mark.

There was nothing more doing that afternoon, but during the next few days of my visit I used the fly exclusively, and found that when properly presented to a rising fish it had a fair chance of acceptance. But with the slightest drag it made a wake like a destroyer, and put the fish down for hours.

It floated well, was easy to see, hooked well and held well. Although it did not catch me a specimen fish, it brought me some thumping baskets, including a 2¾-pounder. Its inventor called it Black Magic. But although it seemed to have occult powers on the Don, its spell was perhaps a local one, for I have not found it so successful elsewhere.

A few evenings ago I was becalmed on a hill loch. The silverhorns were about in thousands and the smaller trout were jumping at them in the air. On these depressing occasions I usually float a Sedge, or a Wickham's Fancy and perhaps catch one, or very rarely two, fish during the evening.

This time I noticed that a few small black chironomids were hatching, and that a few fish were making quiet 'sippy' rises out in the deeper water. I put on a small William's Favourite—just a hook and enough stiff black hackle to float it, a slender black-silk body with a silver rib, and three short black whisks.

During the next hour I took seven trout on that fly, and then a cold wind got up and the fish went down. It must be admitted that three of the fish were under the 10in limit for that loch and had to be returned, but two brace of trout in a flat calm with silverhorns about was something new in my experience.

When, in future, I find the trout fastidious, I shall invoke the powers of darkness. Five centuries of anglers can't be wrong!

September 1960   *Francis Harmar*

Stoneflies for trout

While no angler is required to be an expert on entomology, to take the best out of his sport he should know what he is doing and why he is doing it. In fact he must be something of a scientist as well as an artist, and never more so than when he encounters a hatch of stone-flies.

57

To the chalk-stream man these flies are of little importance; it is only when he goes north or west for a spell of trout-fishing that he will appreciate the part they can play, and properly to seize his opportunity he will soon realise that he must know a little more than can be gleaned from a mere riverside glance. Often he will find them hatching in their thousands, and then they can be very productive of trout, but unless fished in the right way at the right time, equally can they prove exasperating to a degree.

Without going into details of their vagaries and natural history, the angler should know that they belong to the *Plecoptera* order of aquatic flies. To him the importance of this is that, as such, they not only skip any dun stage in their development towards the adult fly, but also they do not pupate. Unlike so many other flies, their life-cycle is reduced to: egg–nymph–fly.

With a few exceptions they are found only in rivers having a fast, pure stream and with rocky or gravel bottoms. Although not entirely absent from waters of the low country, this preference largely confines them to the mountain streams, lochs and lakes of the hilly North and West.

Of some confusion to the visiting angler is that locally they are often called mayflies—a reference to the season of the usual hatches, although this can vary with the species and the locality. In general appearance they resemble the sedges and alders, though their actual structure differs in many ways. There are more than thirty different kinds, but it is only with the large and medium stones the angler need be concerned.

The large stones are brown- or greyish-winged, the two pairs of which, when settled, the flies carry folded flat along their fat, yellowish bodies. Only the female can fly; her mate has but small immature wings which he only occasionally uses by fluttering to help him run from one hiding place to another. The female's flight is slow, untidy, and curiously uncontrolled, and shows little aptitude for manoeuvre. Once seen this helps in riverside identification, as does her marked surface flutter when egg-laying, an action which arouses the typical smashing rise from the feeding trout. Her body is flat and can be more than an inch long, but in flight, having a wing span of double this, she gives an exaggerated impression of size.

The creeper, which is the popular name given to the nymphal stage of the flies, is very active, and seems able to move in any direction. Creepers are usually in hiding except when disturbed. Many species are very destructive to larvae of other flies: a reason why stoneflies are unwelcome in rivers having a nice hatch of *Ephemeroptera*.

The creepers grow rapidly, some moulting as many as 30 times in three years. After the final moult they do not come to the surface for metamorphosis, so there is no nymph rise as in the case of other flies; instead they crawl to the river's edge, where they blow themselves up until the skin bursts and the adult fly emerges.

As flies they live two or three weeks, and although they spend much of their time in hiding beneath stones, rocks and riverside vegetation they can be extremely active. They are strong swimmers, often scampering about the surface of the water, and always in an upstream direction. The general disturbance they create is of great attraction to feeding trout.

So much for a general picture of these curious insects. As I have said, there are something like 30 different species, but fewer than a dozen are of use to the angler. Even to know all these variations is of little, if any, help, the main difference being a matter of size. Many seem to prefer rivers with unstable bottoms, while others like the stones and rocks to be firmly embedded and moss-covered.

One species is of particular interest to the angler, and it is mostly found at high altitudes. This fly also carries a marked yellow stripe which should be in the artificial tyings, in spite of what they say about the colour blindness of trout. It may be that this streak in some way reflects light: I know a fly without it is not so readily taken as one with it. This particular large stone favours low temperatures and will be found on Highland lochs having cold water. It is a good fly with which to dap, as it seems tougher than many of the others.

Another of the large stoneflies, rather dark in colour, is of special interest as it likes an unstable river bed, and one given to hearty spates. The creepers must possess unusual powers of penetration, as on occasion they are forced to bury themselves to great depths to avoid being swept away.

The Usk and parts of the Hereford Wye often produce enormous hatches of these flies, and although in the North June is the best month for them, on these western rivers they are much earlier, and by the second week of June the hatch is over.

Of the smaller stoneflies the yellow sallies and the willow flies are the best known. The common yellow sally favours the more lowland streams, hatching even as far south as Hampshire, and it is very much in evidence on all the Midlands limestone waters. It appears in bursts from April to August, but is not a good trout fly. Only the spent fly seems to have any attraction, and as the female drops her eggs in the late afternoon, fishing the yellow sally means a spent fly late in the day. With the small yellow sally we are back among the hills and mountains. Again it is only the spent fly which interests the trout, but a good tying fished late on a loch having a sandy shore will take fish, especially in July. The willow fly is also too well known to need much description. Its lateness is its main asset; it can put the occasional fish in the bag late in September. That it favours deep water is perhaps the reason for its appearance on such West Country waters as Blagdon, but I have never taken any trout with it there; nor have I seen what could be called 'a rise to the willow'.

Perhaps the smallest of all the stoneflies is that curious needle-like brown fly which always seems to have crept into cracks or the under-side of vegetation. These needle-flies are again late-season flies, and it is only the spent fly which is taken. They can be recognised easily by their disproportionate wing-span. When flying this gives them the appearance of being quite large flies, yet when settled with their long narow wings folded they can be difficult to spot.

June 1957   *G. A. Grattan*

II
Trout

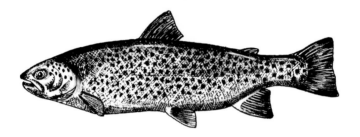

Trout

The late starter

I am 62 years of age and I have a touch of rheumatism in my right shoulder and in my left knee. My eyesight—with the aid of glasses—is not as good as it was. Not the most promising raw material, you might think, for the making of a dry-fly fisherman! But with the arrogance of ignorance, I decided last year to take up fly-fishing for trout when perhaps I should have been thinking of laying it down.

As a boy I had fished for trout in a very famous trout and salmon river in Co Cavan, Ireland, on which my father had a flax mill. My apparatus was of the most primitive—for rod, a stout sapling cut out of the nearest hedge; for line, a hank of cord similar to that used for tying up parcels; and the hook was a monstrous thing that would have done service as a gaff. My 'lure' was the blackhead worm or, when I could get it, the white grub, and occasionally, when the river was in spate, I landed some trout. 'Landed' is the right word, because when these unfortunate fish took my worm or grub I flung up my pole with a mighty heave with the result that the fish either fell off or, if hooked, soared through the air and landed in the bushes.

When these boyhood efforts came to an end I was prevented, as the saying goes, 'by circumstances beyond my control' from doing any more trout fishing until my calling deposited me something over a year ago in a country parish on the banks of the River Main near Ballymena in Northern Ireland. The season was ending as I arrived in late September, but the sight and sound of the river rippling over the stones, and occasionally dappled with the rings of rising trout, aroused irresistible memories and longings.

From October to March I read every book on trout fishing I could find in the local library. Some of them made it all sound very easy, but most of them were decidedly daunting and I very nearly gave it all up and forgot about it. But come March 1 and I decided that at least it was worth a trial.

63

All the fishing books I had read assured me that the beginner can't really learn how to cast a fly from reading about it in a book. How right they were! In spite of preliminary practice on the lawn, my first day on the river was a shattering experience. If the fly, cast and line did not become hooked up or entangled in the grass or bushes behind me, they dropped in a coil at my feet.

The art of depositing a fly a few inches above the nose of a rising fish (which the writers of the fishing books declared to be a 'must') began to look to me as remote and unattainable as a moon landing. But with perseverance and practice some of the absorbed book-learning of the winter started to come through, and fly, cast and line began more often to go more or less in the direction intended.

Then one day it happened! A nice upstream breeze was ruffling the surface of the water; the air was warm and soft but without brilliant sunshine; the trout were rising steadily all over the river. I had 'up' the dry fly which my local tackle-dealer assured me no trout in his senses could resist. I began to cast to a rising fish. As usual my fly was a bit wide of the mark and I was just about to retrieve it and try again when suddenly it vanished from the surface of the water in what the writers describe as a 'boil'.

I was so surprised by this phenomenon that by the time I realised what was happening and 'struck', the trout had ejected the fly and fled into the next parish. But I had had a rise, and it was a turning point. Half an hour or so later the process was repeated, and this time I was more prepared. More by luck than skill, I am sure, my strike this time implanted the hook, and a few minutes later I was gazing with beating heart at my very first trout—all 8oz—caught on a dry fly.

Next to casting, the thing which as a beginner I found most difficult was timing the strike. I missed fish after fish and for a long time had the uneasy suspicion that any that I did connect with had probably already hooked themselves before I intervened.

Then, quite inadvertently, I had a wonderful piece of luck. During a short holiday in a farmhouse in the Mourne Mountains I discovered a small lake which was alive with rudd. As the evening meal at the farmhouse was too late to enable me to return to the nearest trout stream, I decided to spend the remaining hours of daylight fishing for these rudd with worm and paste as I had often done as a boy.

On the first evening at the lake, however, I noticed that many of these fish were rising—just like the trout—to some fly or other which was rising and falling over the lake surface. I hastily removed the worm, hook and float, and put on a trout cast and a dry fly that looked somewhat like the one the fish were rising to. As my first cast landed on the water, which was glassily calm, absolutely nothing happened, though all around the rudd were still busily rising. My fly just lay there on the surface, becalmed, lonely and ignored.

I assumed it must be 'the wrong fly'. But immediately I raised my rod-tip to lift it off the water and substitute another it was instantly snapped up and within a few minutes I had netted my first rudd on a dry fly.

For the remainder of the holiday, each evening for an hour or so until the sun sank behind the Mourne Mountains, I had only to cast my fly—apparently almost any dry fly—give it a slight 'twitch', and instantly it was devoured. Those hours by the lake were superb practice, both in casting and, more particularly, in striking. Even before the holiday ended my percentage of trout hooked to trout risen had begun to improve.

Now my first season as a dry-fly fisherman is past. Looking through my carefully kept records, I find that I caught 30 trout all on the dry fly and of an average weight of 6oz, for an average visit to the river of once a week. I also had some of the most enjoyable and rewardingly pleasant hours I have ever experienced. So if, like me, you get a sudden urge to take up fly-fishing for trout when you are on the wrong side of 60, go ahead and do it! Your only regret will be similar to mine: that it wasn't possible for you to have started much sooner.

March 1973   *J. H. Foy*

That old Test magic

An invitation arrived to fish the upper Test, a magical name for all anglers, but especially for those whose sport is normally on over-fished club and hotel waters. My wife said she would like to come too, even when we woke on the day to find a storm of wind and rain. As we drove down, gloom and despair descended on us at the like-lihood of this wonderful chance being ruined. But we hoped for the proverbial 'fine by eleven'.

At the 10.30 rendezvous with the river-keeper our spirits rose as the wind dropped and the rain eased a little. I started on a carrier and passed by several fish of about a pound. Then, to a more en-couraging rise close to the near bank, I knelt and, with rising excite-ment, I craftily cast an Imperial; it was gently sucked down in the slow-moving water, I tightened, and the fish was on.

Moments later elation turned to horror. Reaching for the net on my hip, I found I had left my scissors dangling from the bag on their piece of string, and this was entangled in the mesh. I tried des-perately to disentangle the scissors with my left hand, still playing the fish with my right. I shouted to my wife who was sheltering in the car; she came running to help and we got the net free and the trout into it. He weighed $2\frac{1}{2}$lb—a good start, and perhaps a sign that this was to be a lucky day.

Who has not plodded fruitlessly along a rough, uneven river-bank, watching the water, hoping for action, and seeing neither trout nor fly? You stumble into holes, tread in cow-pats, and life gets weary. If you're going to be not-catching fish, it would be better on a reser-voir, because you can then use wet flies and at least be casting, doing something, with the angler's eternal optimism of success, sometime. But here, on this miraculous day, fly and fish were showing all the time.

Back on the main river, I broke a hook on an unseen fish, caught and returned a small one, and then spent a long time on an inter-esting problem. A trout was feeding in a small swirl caused by some

66

Summer on the Test, near Fullerton

floating weed caught up on the far bank. The fly would float
naturally for only a moment, and was then dragged by the main
current out of the little bay of weed. But luck held, and after in-
numerable casts the fly had still not caught on the bank nor dragged

so badly as to scare the fish. Eventually, it fell just right, the fish took, and $2\frac{1}{4}$lb more went in the bag.

A grayling came next, not very big, about $\frac{3}{4}$lb, but quite remarkably lively. It fought and jumped as strongly as a trout, although this was still August, when grayling are not usually at their prime.

Further up was a weir-pool, reputed to hold fish which dropped back to the tail to feed. In the fast water it was impossible to see the fish and difficult to see the rises, or a small fly. I tried one of Peter Deane's Terry's Terror, for the ginger hackles float well and are easy to see.

The fly was taken, but the strike produced no more than the line whizzing over my shoulder and catching in a tree behind. The quicker water required a quicker strike, almost instantaneous, not the leisurely affair of the deeper and slower water. After a while a speedier reaction hooked a fish, and we decided to walk back to the hut for our sandwiches.

The sun was now out and our feeling of well-being was heightened by hearing the cry of a kingfisher, and seeing the sparkling flash of two of them as they sped down the river.

Just after lunch we had the most hilarious catch of the day. At the bottom of the beat is a weed-rack, to which cut weed is directed by a stake-and-wire fence running down the middle of the river. Weed floats down one side of this, leaving the other half of the river clear. Standing on the clear-water bank, I saw a rise across in the weed bay. This meant casting over the mid-stream fence, which stood about 18in above the water. Extra hazards were horizontal wires at 4yd intervals, 6in above the water, and connecting the fence to the far bank. Of course, there were also trees behind me.

On such a day one doesn't worry too much about these kind of problems, and soon I was confidently watching the trout sip down my fly. The fish ran upstream and the line caught round one of the vertical angle-irons of the fence. I jumped into the water and flicked the line free. As I regained contact I saw that the leader was bearing against the underside of a horizontal wire upstream.

Nothing broke, however, and the fish turned, tore down past me and began splashing around with line and leader pulling against another of those perishing wires fixed to the other bank. The keeper was nearby and he jumped in, too, and splashed across to take my net. My wife joined the fray with the camera and began asking about exposures and stating where she wanted the fish to be for the best picture. It was quite a busy situation.

That fish ought to have got away. It was more than 2lb and the tip of my leader was only 3lb bs. But the gods were on my side, and the keeper netted it safely.

I suppose a day when one can do no wrong would be too dull. I certainly made mistakes, and I lost fish. But circumstances were favourable and my luck was in, as was proved by the last fish of the day.

It was rising by the far bank under a small willow, some of the branches of which trailed in the water. Casting obliquely across, I could sometimes get the fly on to the water beneath the willow, but more often it caught in an overhanging branch. When I gently handlined, it fell free. This happened several times, but happily I neither lost a fly nor disturbed the trout. However, I could not place the fly further up the tunnel of the willow branches than about level with the trout's back. So I crawled along the bank until I was opposite the guardian willow.

I cast a couple of yards above and beyond the spot where the branch trailed in the water. I reckoned that as the leader was swept against the branch, the fly should be approaching the fish's nose. But it was a one-shot chance, because it would surely not be possible to pull free of the branch without putting the fish down.

Didn't I say it was my lucky day? The trout took the fly, pulled the leader clear of the branch and enabled me to play it out in the open water.

And so, at 6pm, we had the limit of three brace of trout, plus one grayling—14lb of fish to carry back to the car, all caught on the dry fly. What a joy the river had been, with well-tended banks and clear-flowing water. Strategically-placed dams formed pools to break up the shallows on the flatter stretches. The weed was expertly cut in lines, so as to give the fish both cover and open places where they were naturally encouraged to feed on the surface. In such quiet and beautiful surroundings one would have been happy just to be a-fishing. To catch the limit of pink-fleshed wonderful-tasting trout made the day memorable indeed.

January 1971   *Gordon Carlisle*

Sunshine/shadow strategy

'Nothing frightens trout more than moving shadows. In strong slanting sunlight the angler should choose, if possible, to face the sun so that his shadow falls behind him.'

Although not quoted from any particular book on fishing, most anglers will recognise this as typical advice. It is good advice, as far as it goes, especially for beginners. But my object is to discuss the problem of light and shadow in somewhat greater detail and to suggest that this rule-of-thumb is just a little too simple, at least for more advanced anglers. The advice I am about to offer may seem heterodox, but I can quote one excellent contemporary authority to support it.

In the new edition of *A Fly Fisher's Life*, Charles Ritz gives this advice on fishing the evening rise: 'As soon as day declines . . . take up a position on the bank with the light behind you, which is the only way of watching the presentation and the taking of your fly.'

First consider the angler's point of view. If he is fishing into the light, everything coming between him and the sun tends to be in silhouette, without detail. This applies to any break on the surface of the water. A ripple or a rise will be a dark lump on the water. Often the one cannot be distinguished from the other, and a rise may be missed.

Peering into the sun is quite painful and very indiscriminating. Between the angler and the westering sun there is likely to be a blinding pathway across the water into which a floating fly just disappears. The angler will find himself craning his neck first to one side and then to the other to shorten the 'blind' period of the fly's passage across the glare. How often the best fish of the day is lost at the moment of the angler's blindness! Furthermore, when the angler faces the light, the surface becomes impenetrable to sight.

Fish activity underwater at any distance becomes wholly invisible. Nymph-fishing thus loses one of its most favourable circumstances. On the other hand, at early dawn or late evening, facing the light can give the angler one of his most enjoyable experiences, a mysterious view of a watery world into which he cannot see but from which comes unexpected excitement. And he may prefer the suddennesses of fishing against the light even at the cost of some success.

Polarising glasses, of course, will mitigate the inconvenience. They save eye-strain by removing much of the reflected glare. But they also reduce the total amount of light available for vision.

Now consider the trout's view. It doesn't enjoy bright light in its eyes any more than the angler. Having no eyelids, it can neither blink nor peer. When the sun is high and bright it illuminates the bottom and the trout naturally looks in the direction of easier vision or else 'sleeps', with its attention switched off until something stimulating excites it again.

In these bright midday conditions, the trout frequently shows a comparative lack of skill in intercepting surface food; it misses or rises short. It, too, has blind spots caused by the light in its eyes; whereas at the beginning or end of the day, when the slanting light is weakened, the trout can take things from the surface with maximum precision when they come within its field of special attention.

On cloudy days, when the light is evenly filtered and seems to come from no particular direction, the trout's attention is less specialised. Any object coming towards it either on its left or its right will command its active interest. But when the light has a definite point of origin, the trout will direct its attention down-light rather than the other way.

71

One eye will be shielded from the direct rays, and objects in its field of attention will be brightly illuminated, including the angler and his polished rod, which will heliograph warnings straight to the eye of the fish. The trout's other eye, looking up-light, will be much less efficient. Objects in its field (comparatively a field of inattention) will appear in silhouette or merged into the darker background.

This theory of the trout's contrasting fields of attention and in-attention in conditions of slanting light is surely a reasonable one. Attention is a normal brain function in the process of perception. The trout, with its unshielded eyes, has special need of such means of avoiding the effects of glare. Not that this is its only protection.

The trout's eyes are constantly bathed in cool water and need no saving tears. Water is less transparent to light than air and the trout can increase its protection against glare by sinking deeper, but only at the expense of discrimination, since it is a short-sighted creature. In shallow water, or when it chooses to swim high and near the surface, the trout is less handicapped by short-sight. In fact, in these circumstances, when its field of attention is most specialised, it can see movements as far off as 20 or even 30yd.

Surely, therefore, it would be wiser for the angler to choose to position himself in the field of the trout's inattention rather than the other; that is, to fish with the light coming from behind him and towards the trout.

To do this, which is in contradiction of the simple rule-of-thumb usually advocated, has one special advantage. It gives the angler his best vision into the water. At the distance of his flies he may be able to observe the take or detect what Skues taught us to look for when nymphing, 'the little brown wink underwater'.

Nevertheless, it must be admitted that fishing down the light has its special disadvantage. It throws the angler's shadow in front of him over the water he desires to fish. I maintain, however, that this difficulty is rather an exaggerated one and need not handicap the angler if he is fully aware of it and acts suitably. He can minimise the handicap in several ways—by taking advantage of high banks, bushes, or trees in whose greater shadows his own may be swallowed. He can reduce the length of his shadow by keeping low or wading deep, by casting a longer line than usual so as to reach beyond his shadow, or by horizontal casting so as to avoid his rod shadow falling on the fishing area.

Some of these methods are not possible on narrow streams, when the original simple rule-of-thumb may be the only resource. But there are other variations on this problem.

It seldom happens that the angler casts a shadow directly in line with his cast. Fortunately, it often falls at a pronounced angle to the flow of the stream, and if this angle is in the other quarter from that in which he wishes to fish then he has a larger sweep of water available. An angle of 45 degrees in one direction will give him 90 degrees or more in the other, with every possibility of success. He must move slowly all the time.

Trout are not frightened so much by the shadow *per se* as by its sudden appearance or movement. A slowly-moving shadow will cause, at most, a nervous reaction in its vicinity, but is unlikely to cause a spread of contagious fear, as happens when terrified fish flee into neighbouring areas.

I have often fished a pool successfully, my shadow slowly following the path of my flies as I proceeded downstream from cast to cast. Something similar is possible when upstream dry-fly fishing, except that the angle of shadow has to be in the other direction.

Apart from these tactics to avoid casting shadow, there are two others that have to do with the trout's fields of attention and inattention. They are especially important for the dry-fly fisher when he has marked down his fish or knows its probable lie.

It is a great advantage to present the fly in the fish's field of attention. This means that when the angler faces the light, he should drop the fly on the near side of the fish. This is a special recommendation for the rule-of-thumb, since the tactic then is fairly easy and the trout has every chance of seeing only the fly because it is near it: the nylon is further away and less likely to be noticed.

73

When the angler has the light behind him, ideally he should drop the fly on the far side of the fish, because that is its field of attention. Of course, there is a real danger of lining the fish and, in this case, the curved cast, which brings the fly to the fish ahead of the nylon, is the supreme tactic.

Finally, let me reassure beginners, or those who think my suggestions are only for the very skilful, that the ideal is not necessary for successful fishing down-light. Wind and current often co-operate by providing a broken surface to the water. Not only do ripples and current help to obscure the attachments, but they also break up shadows, another reason why we should not be bound to the simple rule-of-thumb.

February 1967   *C. R. Pearce*

When a loch is dour

Every fisherman knows only too well the days when a loch seems lifeless, and lunch-time, after four hours of hard work by two rods, shows nothing in the boat and the net still dry. It is very disappointing and, to make matters worse, quite often happens on some famed water when the long-awaited visit comes off.

Local boatmen will be full of excuses and suggestions, the former possibly thinly veiled criticism of methods and the latter mainly how last week's anglers had amazing catches each day. But if no boatman is aboard, and the rods are strangers to the water, experiments must be made if the afternoon is to wipe out the sad memory of the morning.

Usually no signs of trout have been seen at all—no rises, despite what fly is on the water—and the visitors may doubt that the loch is as good as its reputation promises. Maybe one monster has been seen in the air, away out in mid-loch during the morning, its return to the water signalled by an impressive crash. But this is an old one among loch trout, and is famous for keeping the customers interested.

For the afternoon programme, a change of method can be tried,

Trouting of another kind: Dartmoor's rocky West Dart, a short distance above the
mouth of the Swincombe River

and here are a few of the possibilities. A big fly on the tail can be tried. A really big one, a size 8 or 6—even a double-hooked salmon fly sometimes works. It may be the sight of a really large mouthful, or it may be merely the fact that it sinks the cast deeply and quickly, but sometimes this does start things moving. And quite often it is the small flies on the droppers that are taken.

The sinking of the cast may be the answer. On a windy day, when the boat is drifting quickly, this is often a good plan, for in these conditions it is difficult to sink a nylon cast far enough before it must be recovered.

Failing a big fly, a gut cast can be tried, for gut does sink more quickly than nylon. Small, double-hooked flies, as used on Loch Leven, can also be tried, much of their success being due to the speed with which they sink the cast.

On some lochs the Worm-fly is the only thing that hooks anything, and one or two should be carried. These are best when tied with wire instead of nylon as the connecting link between the two flies, and should always have red tape. The curious thing about the Worm-fly is that on some waters it does best on the tail, fished deeply, while on others it is most effective on the bob and is taken on the surface, often close to the boat as the cast is being recovered.

If the water is very dark, as on many hill-lochs in peaty areas, sometimes a sea-trout lure, such as is used for estuary fishing, will hook trout when normal flies are ignored. The two-hook type is better than the three-hook for this purpose. The Demon, Alexandra and Yellow Peril dressings are better, too, than the blue colouring. Although on Loch Leven the boatmen often suggest these as the tail fly on a four-fly cast, when the day has been a poor one, it will be found that on other lochs the best results are obtained when the lure is fished alone on the cast.

Moving into the realm of local superstition is the resort to a drop of oil of cinnamon on the flies. It sounds crazy, but it does work, sometimes, although only once with real effect in my own experience. Some keen and successful loch fishers swear by this strange habit,

76

The quiet hills: fishing for brown trout on Loch Cama, Sutherland

and keep a cinnamon lozenge in cast-box or wallet.

A more useful and understandable change is to put on a cast of the sparsely-dressed Clyde flies. But the frequent success of these bare-looking objects on some lochs ties up with the times when a battered and bedraggled fly has proved the best of the day's offerings. In most cases trout flies are dressed far too heavily, and some trimming with a pair of scissors is usually an improvement.

If equipment is limited, as it may well be if the water is an inaccessible hill-loch and the minimum quantity of gear has been hauled up the long path to it, a simple and sometimes forgotten variation is to work the cast much more than usual. Some hours of inaction tend to bring on lazy rod-work, and automatic casting and recovery never does much good. A hooked trout usually wakes up the angler and casting improves for a while, but if no such welcome diversion occurs, it is best to pause for a flask-break and then make a fresh start in a more energetic manner. Work the flies craftily, as though a trout could be seen below in the dark water, approaching a moving insect instead of avoiding a lifeless-looking object hanging almost motionless below the surface.

If the wind strengthens, a form of what may be called modified dapping can be tried, without the usual equipment of long, light rod and a blow-line. Making up a cast with one of the biggest and most bushy flies available, such as Black Pennell, Blue Zulu or Soldier Palmer, a fair enough imitation of dapping can be carried out. A cigarette paper on the line can help to provide extra wind resistance to take the fly out. If the wind is really strong, the fly will dap on the wave tops and trout may take the enticing offering quite close to the boat. This is best tried late in the day, and the fly, cast and some feet of the line should be greased to avoid drowning the fly if cast and line touch the water.

These suggestions may do some good when a blank morning has soured the angler. At any rate, they give the impression that something is being tried, and prevent the hopeless, let's-give-it-up feeling from developing. They are not intended for days when trout are seen, but not hooked; they are intended for the times when visiting anglers, new to the water, begin to doubt if it holds any trout at all.

September 1958   '*Alexandra*'

Bad weather in spring

When March goes out like a lion and the first days of the trout season? 'Give the trout a chance to get into condition,' they say. at home waiting for a favourable change in the weather? Are you one of those virtuous folk who settle for the prevailing market and write to the angling Press recommending further delays in the start of the season? 'Give the trout a chance to get into condition', they say. 'The middle of April is early enough.'

If so, you are unlike your grandfather. He had no advantage of modern rain-proof clothing, and yet it was the February Red rather than the Large Spring Olive that specially interested him in his first ventures to the river. If I agree that his zeal was excessive and premature, I cannot agree that the beginning of April is too early. Long before opening day my rod is varnished, reel oiled, and ever-hopeful modifications of Blue Duns and Olives are already tied on the latest brand of nylon. Whatever the weather, I'm off to the river on the first available day of the season. I suppose warm and sunny bee-buzzing spring is what I chiefly hope for. On such a day, at precisely half past one, trout and grayling will come on the rise. That's what I expect, and it's glorious in prospect.

But what if the weather refuses? What if there is an abrupt return to winter with wet, squally and miserable days? Do you stay at home? I don't. Frequent experience has taught me to rejoice in the prospect of an exciting day at the expense of numbed fingers and eyes blinded with snowflakes. Instead of one thrilling half-hour rise with blank beginning and end to the day, I expect offers at any time and a much heavier bag to carry home at the end.

My earliest recollection of such a beginning to the season is of fly-fishing as a boy from the shore of a local reservoir, half of which was private and half public. The bright morning sky soon clouded over and a strong wind sprang up. Then came the snow, heavy and wet. I was forced to retreat to the shelter of pine trees that grew down to the water's edge in the private sector. Before the keeper found me

The Borders in spring—and St Mary's Loch, where Stoddart used to fish with the 'Ettrick Shepherd'

there I had landed five trout and was getting offers at every other cast. The keeper was sympathetic and did not put me off. Perhaps he was too astonished that a boy should persist in such unpleasant conditions. On two succeeding days I returned and in exactly similar weather made similar catches. These were exceptional successes at an early age and left an indelible prejudice in favour of bad weather in spring.

Two springs ago I spent the first week of April on the Tweed. In very mixed weather I had good catches every day, the best times being when the weather got 'worse'. On those days my flies continued to interest the trout until nearly eight in the evening.

Four springs ago, again on the Tweed, I had five days of terrible weather. I wore consistently two pairs of trousers in my waders and an anorak topped with a gas cape. I kept dry and by my activity quite warm. I enjoyed every bad day of it and have seldom landed so many fish. I say landed, because I returned the largest fish that were too big for my frying-pan. It was on this memorable holiday that I first theorised about the why and the wherefore of good fishing in bad spring weather.

I noticed that on very cold days the temperature actually rises when the sky clouds over. Rain or even snow, however uncomfortable to the fisher, may be a symptom of this change in temperature, which they convey to the water. The dull light which prevails at such times is an additional or alternative explanation. In such light one seldom experiences short rises. Almost every offer is a take. This indicates confidence on the part of the fish and this confidence may be due to clear vision (which I think is most likely in subdued but evenly filtered light), or else to nymphal activity which stimulates the feeding responses of the trout. I favour the effect of light on the trout rather than on the nymphs, for I have not observed much hatching of fly on such occasions. I have used the term 'rise' but more often than not the take is an unobserved underwater pull.

What flies are appropriate on such days of wild spring weather? The Large Spring Olive or the Iron Blue Dun are obvious choices. I prefer my own tyings (which change experimentally each year with little obvious effect either way) of the Greenwell and the Gold-ribbed Hare's Ear. The Greenwell is good in any form. But I prefer it as a nymph on a long-shank hook, slightly leaded. The Hare's Ear I now make from the fur of my Abyssinian cat. This fly seems to be attractive to small spring-salmon as well as trout. I've hooked one or two every spring in recent years and landed some of them.

So, if spring comes in like winter, don't write to the Press about the season starting too soon. Go out and enjoy the good bad weather and the exciting fishing it may bring. If you are concerned about the condition of the trout, you can acquire virtue by returning the big fish to fatten up for the summer. There will be plenty of well-mended medium fish to gladden your heart and your stomach. Be brave and enjoy the inclemency of spring.

March 1965   *C. R. Pearce*

A theory of light

The art of angling is, admittedly, an art in deception. The fly-fisherman, for his part, seeks to present an artificial, either on or under the surface of the water, in such a manner as to deceive the trout. But the art of angling is also the art of catching fish and it is surely carrying deception a little too far if a fly is virtually invisible to the creature it was designed not only to deceive but to hook. Nevertheless, many anglers offer to trout, season after season, artificial flies which, because of the prevailing conditions of light, are extremely well camouflaged—from the fish!

I have come, through the years, greatly to respect the memory of an old fisherman who, believing it to be of paramount importance that the trout should see the fly, translated a simple theory of light into practice with telling results.

His theory may be simply stated. Imagine a trout swimming in limpid water on a bright, sunny day. It sees in its 'window' a fly. Does the fly appear to the fish as a light object or a dark one? Surely we have reason on our side if we think it must appear dark, for bright sunlight, especially when the fly is between the fish and the sun, makes the recognition of colour difficult. On the other hand, a dull day, giving conditions of diffused light, would enable the fish to discern the actual colour of the fly more clearly. Furthermore, in poor light, it is natural to assume that a dark fly would be less visible than a light one. He also concluded, reasonably as far as human experience is concerned, that since at dusk a most conspicuous colour to man is white, herein lies, at least in part, the attraction of the Coachman.

Before the above paragraph is dismissed by such a question as, 'What enables a sea trout to find the blackest fly on the blackest night?' and by the time-honoured phrase, 'Bright day—bright fly, dull day—dark fly', let me place on the other side of the scales an illustration which at least speaks volumes for fishing a fly in contrast to the colour of its surroundings. And let it be noted that I am particularly referring to daytime fishing for brown trout in fast streams.

One sunny day in April an angler on the River Tamar was using a light March Brown. He caught no fish during the hour before midday. After lunch he noticed that conditions had become brighter than ever and changed his fly to an Alder with a body of black ostrich herl and a dark grouse wing. Soon he caught a fish—and he went on to land no fewer than nine others, all on the same pattern and all while the bright light lasted. As the natural alder makes but a sporadic appearance on the water in question and generally not until June, he concluded that it was the dark fly against the bright light that had attracted the trout. This conclusion I find perfectly reasonable.

Although in the streams of Devonshire, the Blue Upright is perhaps the best all-round fly to use throughout the season, the Blue Dun with its pale starling-wing and lighter-blue hackle is probably an even better fly in the opening weeks. May not the reason for this be that early in the season, when the days, and certainly the waters, are less bright, the paler fly shows up better? When the sun comes out and the stickles sparkle, by all means put up a Blue Upright—and note that the correct dressing of the hackle is an extremely dark steely-blue which could almost be described as black!

There is at least one other consideration in making a fly visible in conditions of bright light. Apart from choosing it for an overall dark appearance, it is often advantageous to have, particularly in a wet fly, a fairly plump though well-defined body. There is no material which gives a better combination of these qualities than peacock or ostrich herl.

Most of my fishing is now done in Devon and Cornwall, and here the rivers tend to be fast. Working on the theory that if a trout does not see my fly it can take no interest in it whatsoever, I mentally put most of my patterns into two categories—'Flies for bright conditions' and 'Flies for dull conditions'. When I can discern no known fly on the water—and this is often—I have recourse on cloudy days to light patterns such as Silver March Browns, Half Stones, Blue Duns and Red Uprights, the last having wings of starling or a light-blue head-hackle. On a sunny day I select from dark-hackled March Browns, Pheasant Tails with badger-hackle, Blue Uprights with dark hackle, and the Coch-y-Bonddu. At dusk I trust the white wing of the Coachman, but on light nights and in low water I fish its plump peacock-herl body with a shortened white wing.

August 1964   *Frederick Mold*

Learn to cast a long line

It is sad but true that it is the most experienced river fly-fisher who seems to have the most difficulty in dealing with the problems that reservoir fishing poses. The coarse-fish angler who decides to sample reservoir fly-fishing has much to learn but little to forget. He does not expect to catch much while he is learning, and he is delighted when he lands a fish or two.

The skilled river trout-fisher, on the other hand, is often liable to expect his expertise to bring him success on a reservoir; to be dis-appointed at failure; and to be slow to accept that successful reser-voir fly-fishing involves different equipment and different methods from those used in river fishing. If he has come to regard any devia-tion from river-fishing tackle and tactics as unsportsmanlike, he may find his visits to reservoirs not only fruitless, but altogether distasteful.

Let us consider practical details. The rather short, delicate rod and light double-taper line that is suitable for river fishing is not very satisfactory for reservoir work. This apparatus is designed for accurate casting at distances of, say, 10 to 15yd, and to be capable of putting a fly down lightly at such ranges. In skilful hands it is capable of throwing perhaps 18yd in favourable conditions.

On a river 15 to 18yd looks a long throw. On even a small reservoir it looks a very short distance indeed. The river-fisher does not under-stand that there is a kind of optical illusion. He thinks that for some obscure reason he is casting badly—'off form' or something of that

The sun goes down over London's own trout reservoir—the Queen Mother Reservoir at Datchet; in the distance, Windsor Castle

kind. His only notion of extending range being to put more of his full double-taper line into the air, he soon gets into trouble, with more line out than his rod can control.

It is necessary on most reservoirs, and desirable on all of them, to acquire more suitable equipment. There is a wide choice, and reservoir experts can argue indefinitely about what is best. I would feel handicapped without a rod that can handle 30yd of number 7 line (AFTM rating). For very long casting, using big flies and lures, a rod capable of handling 36yd of number 9 line can often confer considerable advantages; in all cases, lengths of from 9ft to 9ft 6in help to keep the back-cast clear of bank-side vegetation, especially when the angler is wading knee-deep.

There is no doubt that the shooting-head system has great advantages, correctly used. All the objections to the basic system are nonsense, though some of them are true of misuses and misconceptions.

I most strongly advise anyone who has a river-fly-fishing background and who wants to catch trout from reservoirs to seek competent advice about long casting, because without it he will be at a grave disadvantage. A man can be a beautiful short-range caster, possessing tremendous accuracy and delicacy, and able to catch great numbers of fish from rivers, and yet be a hopeless bungler on a reservoir, where it may be necessary to cast 30 or even 40yd to reach the fish.

I have often read articles and letters in angling journals that deprecate long casting and say that it is unnecessary and that fish can be caught at modest ranges from reservoirs. So they can, sometimes, but more often they cannot. A man who can cast 40yd can fish at 20yd with little effort when 20yd is sufficient. A man whose limit of range is 20yd is working hard all the time he is casting that far, and if the trout are upwards of 30yd away he cannot possibly catch any. Learning to cast 40yd places no man under an obligation never to cast less distance!

I am well convinced that, while it takes much more than just the ability to cast a long way to be successful at catching reservoir trout, there is no other single thing that will increase the catch so much as the capability of casting a really long line easily and without expenditure of great energy and effort.

The next step that the experienced river-fisher has to take is that of mastering the art of using sunken as well as floating lines. Often the trout are near the bottom and nowhere near the surface. To catch them it is necessary to fish deep. That can sometimes be done by using a long leader in conjunction with a floating line and a very slow retrieve. More often, especially on the bigger reservoirs, the more productive technique is to use one of the range of sinking lines, so as to allow a faster retrieve.

I like to carry a floating line, a slow-sinker and a high-density fast-sinker, and in the course of a day's fishing I usually have occasion to wet all three. Lack of space prevents me enlarging on the importance of correctly judging how much time to allow a fly to sink, and at what rate and in what manner to retrieve it after it has sunk to the correct depth. These things are governed by the kind of fly chosen, the depth of water, the behaviour of the fish, the force and direction of the wind and many other factors. The river-fisher must understand that it isn't just a matter of chucking the fly out and dropping it in again, but that he has a whole new art to learn.

One other matter is frequently overlooked—correct choice of leader. The river-fisher will generally be well enough equipped with a 7ft 6in to 9ft leader, tapered to whatever point thickness is appropriate to the river he fishes. His range of fly sizes will be, perhaps, 12 to 16 or 17. Except for the mayfly season, one leader length and point strength will suffice for all his fishing.

On a reservoir, his fly may be anything from a number 16 Midge Pupa to a lure tied on two or three tandem hooks as big as a number 8 or even a number 6. He must therefore learn that a substantial change in fly size has to be matched by an appropriate change in his leader. You cannot successfully fish a number 16 fly on a 12lb leader point, nor a tandem number 8 lure on a 3lb point. Leader length is also important. To get, say, a Corixa down 12ft, with a floating fly-line, needs a 15ft leader, but you can't fish that against a strong breeze. So, to catch fish, it frequently becomes necessary to adjust both the length and strength of the leader.

Few river flies are of any use on reservoirs, so a new selection has to be acquired. Every experienced reservoir angler would probably offer a different list of favourite patterns. Here is mine:

SWEENEY TODD in sizes 12, 8 and tandem size 8 lure.

CHURCH FRY otherwise known as Squirrel and Orange, in sizes 8 and tandem size 8.

INVICTA, size 12, standard dressing, and with bluish-green body and body hackle.

MALLARD AND CLARET, sizes 10 and 12.

MIDGE PUPA imitations, black, olive, green, orange and red, sizes 10–16.

CORIXA, sizes 10 and 12.

WORM-FLY, sizes 8, 10, 12.

BLACK AND PEACOCK SPIDER, sizes 10 and 12.

POLYSTICKLE, size 6, long-shank, brown back, orange hackle: and orange back, orange hackle. Also size 12 with white polythene body, brown back.

AYLOTT'S ORANGE, size 12.

BUFF SEDGE, dry, size 12, normal shank.

RED SEDGE, dry, size 10, long shank.

GROUSEWING SEDGE, dry, size 12, normal shank.

DADDY-LONG-LEGS, dry, size 10, long shank.

One could treble this list and still include useful dressings only, but the above provides a good selection for an angler new to reservoir work.

April 1970   *Richard Walker*

Trouting in moorland streams

Every trout-fishing season has its lessons to teach in retrospect, and one of the most valuable lessons to those who suffered the drought conditions which last season afflicted large parts of Scotland and Ireland was the changes which occurred in the habitat of the trout as the waters fell.

All moorland and rain-fed streams are characterised by their rapid rise and fall and the consequent movement of trout from pools to shallows when the water level permits, and back again when the stream subsides. Last year the period during which many rivers had subsided was prolonged, and it was therefore necessary to search out the best lies. The results were valuable and give a good lead to tactics which may be gainfully employed during more normal summer weather when rivers shrink temporarily.

It was soon found that the textbook positions of trout, such as the tails of pools, immediately before boulders where the bed tends to be scooped out, and in the smooth glides between broken water, were unfrequented by sizable fish. Some of these situations, indeed, were either laid bare or reduced to a water depth so low that even if occupied by a fish, the trout was too easily alarmed to be fishable.

Fishing these classic marks, if they could be found, was merely a source of irritation in that they were frequented, if at all, by under-sized trout. On the other hand, by carefully searching out the new haunts taken up by the larger fish, it was often possible to make contact with fish of surprisingly good weight considering the low level of the river. The basic consideration in the approach to what may be termed drought conditions is that as a river falls, the number of places of sufficient depth, cover and food-supply available to the trout is greatly diminished. To a considerable extent the fish tend to live much more crowded lives than when the river is full and when each can choose its own holt. It is worthwhile, therefore, after taking a sizable fish to try the same area again after a suitable interval in the hope that another of the company will be interested. This applies particularly to pools of any area or to deep runs under banks. If in fishing up a mile or so of river one finds three or four places that yield results, it is usually good practice to start at the bottom of the beat and try again the few areas that were fruitful.

Apart from the more obvious places that will appeal to the fisher-man who has studied the movement of the fish and realises the kind of water he is looking for, there are three distinct formations, common to practically all fast-running streams, that will repay attention. The first is the fair-sized pool which, when the river is full, is deep and in which the stream moves heavily. When the water drops, usually one side of the pool becomes very shallow and little more than an eddy. The other side—unless the inlet is almost exactly central, which is seldom the case—takes the main flow of the water. Not only is the bed worn away, giving depth, but the bank is eroded, providing cover for the fish. The volume of water will not only provide a

89

comparatively well-aerated stream, but will carry with it most of the available food supply.

These runs should always be fished methodically from the tail upwards, if possible, but if not, then across. They frequently harbour some of the best trout in the area. Generally, such runs are best fished with a dry fly cast well under the bank. As the bank itself is usually of earth, without any serious obstruction, it often pays to cast the fly against the bank so that it falls on to the water immediately below.

The second type of water which often yields results may appear unpromising at first sight. This is the bankside eddy from the main stream often covered with natural white foam. These eddies are often fairly deep as a result of the constant swirl of water, are often over-hung by trees or bushes, and are a favourite resort of sizable fish. Such fish cruise in the eddies and appear to find a good deal of food in and just below the white surface foam. Here it has been found that a fly which just penetrates the surface film is often successful.

A quite different proposition is the quiet, almost still, reach between pools or broken runs, where there may be a thick growth of reeds at the sides. If there is any breeze a dry fly cast as near as possible to the reeds and allowed to remain riding the wavelets will often bring up a fish. But a more effective technique is to cast a large nymph close to, and as near parallel as possible with, the reeds and allow it to sink as far as is judged wise to avoid fouling the roots. It should then be retrieved in short draws until it reaches the surface. Some surprisingly large fish for moorland streams have been taken in this way.

June 1969   *B. W. C. Cooke*

Loch Tay on a day in spring

Three size 12 Teal and Silver and three size 14 . . . the same of Blae and Black . . . now what else do I need?

It is a particular pleasure to me to sort out flies and arrange casts in preparation for a fishing trip. My selection of flies is made after reference to my fishing diary, in which is recorded every outing I have been on over the past 25 years. A non-angling acquaintance once asked me if my diary listed bad days as well as good days. I told him that fishing trips were like the various brands of Scotch whisky: some were good, some were better, but none was bad.

Apart from the practical information regarding flies, tactics and weather conditions, keeping a diary means that I can relive each and every one of those wonderful days spent on river and loch.

As I thumb through the pages I can see that since returning from the Army in 1947 I have topped the century of days on Loch Tay. This beautiful Perthshire loch stretches from Killin in the west to the lovely black-and-white cottaged village of Kenmore 14 miles to the east. The northern shoreline is dominated by the mighty mass of Ben Lawers which rears its rugged peak almost 4,000ft into the clouds.

I have fished along almost the entire length of this picturesque loch, but my favourite stretch in spring is about halfway along the northern bank, around the mouth of the Lawers Burn. When a brisk south-west wind sends waves scurrying across the water, the plump trout of Loch Tay are to be found close to the bank of the rocky bays which dot this part of the loch.

It was on a day such as this that I stood on the shingle just about 100yd east of the old deserted clachan of Lawers. The sun was shining, but there was a chill in the air to remind one that winter hadn't waved its last good-bye. The water level was slightly up, and that usual tremor of anticipation made my senses excitingly aware of every slap of the waves on the stony shore. I had several casts prepared, and my only problem was to decide whether the waves were high enough to merit a size 12 hook or if I would stick to my usual size 14.

The wind was gusting quite strongly, and this persuaded me to favour the larger size. As I tied on the tapered cast, 5lb down to 3lb nylon, my eyes were already searching out the tree-girt bay that would be my starting point. The flies I was using were all old reliable

91

There's more to fishing . . . birch, bracken and upper Tay glisten in the sun as
storm clouds gather over Glen Lyon

favourites—Teal and Silver on tail, Mallard and Claret and Blae and Black as mid-flies, with Woodcock and Mixed on the bob. They had all performed well on numerous occasions and fully earned their position as front-line attackers. I waded in to just above knee-height and sent them searching out at an angle of 45 degrees to the line of the waves. My day had begun.

As is usual in spring, I fished fairly slowly, allowing the flies to sink and bringing them in with gentle pulls of about a foot of line at a time. The first offer came quite soon, but either my reflexes were still in first gear or the fish wasn't really in earnest, because it was *chug*, *splutter*, and then that sickening slack line. I had a quick look at my cast, and then back to the fray. This aperitif had quickened my pulse-rate and it was with increased eagerness that I plied the water.

Halfway down the bay an old split-trunk birch tree lurches drunkenly towards the loch. I have had many a trout just opposite this landmark was well prepared when a savage tug sent the raised rod-point plunging. Soon a good half-pounder was in the creel. The Mallard and Claret was first to score, but the Blae and Black took the next three fish as I worked my way, four or five paces at a time, along the loch. They were typical Loch Tay trout— between 6oz and 10oz, and strong fighters, with a wildness inherited from generations of free ancestors.

I stopped for a flask of hot soup and a sandwich around midday and, as the wind had softened a shade, I changed my cast to a similar one with size 14 hooks. The sun was now fairly warm and I could see it glistening on the snow-capped peak of the Ben. There's a wee loch up there called Lochan nan Cat. It lies just below and to the north-east of the summit at an altitude of 2,200ft. It holds a lot of small trout, but July is the month to try for them.

I continued my way along the loch picking up fish in almost every bay. The Woodcock and Mixed did not produce any results, so I replaced it with a Dark Partridge and Orange Spider. This also proved fruitless, but I reasoned that the cold wind was keeping the fish well down and my bob fly wasn't quite reaching them. The Teal

93

and Silver accounted for only two trout, although, as is usual with this fly, they were the heaviest. One was a good fish of 1lb 2oz, but the other, around the 1½lb mark, was thin and not well mended, so I returned it gently to the water.

I finished up that day just below Cragganruar and almost exactly opposite the deepest part of the loch. It had been a good day and my diary records the take-home catch as nine trout weighing 5lb 2oz. The fly score, counting returned fish was: Teal and Silver—two; Mallard and Claret—three; Blae and Black—six; with Woodcock and Mixed and Dark Partridge and Orange Spider having no success at all.

I remember the walk back along the lochside as the later afternoon grew colder. I made a detour up by Machuim to drop in a brace of trout to Donald Campbell and his good lady. Their house stands 300ft above the loch and commands a glorious view of the whole area. Donald's soft Highland voice and gentle manner cloak the purposeful strength and skill with which he farms this wild country. Both he and his wife have always a cheery welcome for visiting hill-walkers and anglers.

Dropping back down to the road, I tramped on to where I had left the car. Then I was off. Down past Kenmore to Aberfeldy, up through the Sma' Glen to Crieff and on to the bustling flurry of the industrial belt of Scotland. My fishing day was ended, but I had still to record the facts and details which would ensure that it would not be forgotten.

April 1977   *Peter Reid*

Irish trout on salmon flies

I have just been on an Irish fishing holiday and, perhaps like too many fishermen, I simply cannot resist the urge to talk about it. Still, some of it was very interesting from a fishing point of view.

The idea was to fish the dry fly for gillaroo trout on the Drowes river, which drains Lough Melvin into the sea. What a wonderful

94

An Irish gillaroo. Jimmy Murphy, a boatman on Lough Mask, with a fine four-pounder

river it is! But more of that later. When we arrived there was scarcely any of it left, because of the drought. The gillaroo trout had moved up into the cooler and deeper waters of the lough itself, so we had to seek our sport elsewhere. And the chief lesson we learned was that in trout fishing there is infinite scope for experiment.

New techniques can be found out every day, and new ways of catching trout. Take Lough Erne, the great lough just north of the Ulster border. Lough Erne trout are quarries to dream about. The particular boat I fished from had accounted for a fourteen- and an eleven-pounder within the last month. And this was no exception.

There is, of course, a drawback to these wonderful trout. They seldom rise to flies except at mayfly-time. Then they take the dapped insect and the spent gnat. Afterwards they can occasionally be caught in the evening on an imitation of the Great Red Sedge or Murragh, but not often. Until recently, few people thought of fishing for them during the daytime in summer or autumn, except by trolling a minnow or spoon. Yet now, flies are the most popular lures—thanks entirely to an experiment made by a boatman.

This is not fly-fishing in its usual sense, because the flies are salmon flies and they are trolled. But nevertheless, the boatman made a discovery—and all discoveries are important. One day, after many fruitless hours of trolling the spoon, he advised his fishermen to tie on some salmon flies which they had with them. They caught nine trout immediately. News does not take long to spread, and today the spoon has given way to the salmon fly. The big trout are being caught to an extent which is even giving the Board of Conservators some cause for worry. However, the trout seem as plentiful and as big as ever.

The interesting thing is why were these flies so successful? The answer, as nearly always, lies in the natural food of the trout. The lough is full of perch, and the trout feed greedily on the perch fry. Sometimes, during the latter end of the season, the perch fry come up to the surface and the big trout follow them. They appear to find that a salmon fly looks more like a perch fry than does a spoon.

96

At any rate, the gulls seem to support this view. Gulls eat the perch fry, too. In fact, if you see gulls hovering over the water, that will be a good spot to fish, because they will be hovering over the perch fry and over the trout that chase them. Quite often, they will hover over your own flies, as you troll them 30yd or so behind the boat. They will even pick up your own flies from the water, whereas I have never heard of them picking up a spoon.

So the flies appear to be excellent imitations of natural food. But all in all, this trolling of flies is a soul-destroying business. You sit in a boat which chugs round the lough under the power of an outboard motor. You troll with four rods, using tough nylon, and when one of the rods strikes a trout, you simply wind the fish in. That is all. Unless the trout is over 3lb, the boat does not even stop.

It is, I suppose, a nice restful sport. But the only fishing excitement comes when you play a large fish. Despite the strong tackle, a trout in double figures is very exciting indeed. Then the boat stops, the other three rods are reeled in, and you have a long battle on your hands. We caught quite a few nice trout, but it was not our luck to capture a really big one. I lost a big one, after some time, at the side of the boat.

Probably it served me right for turning temporarily into a trophy hunter. The boatman philosophically remarked that it was just as well that I had lost the fish. He said: 'When people first come here, they want a 6lb trout. When they've caught it, they want a ten-pounder. After that, a fifteen-pounder . . .'

We left Lough Erne to other trophy hunters, feeling rather ashamed of ourselves and wishing that we had been there to fish it at the right time of the year, when the huge trout feed on natural insects. It is perhaps worth relating that we often caught two good trout on the same team of flies, one on the tail fly and one on the dropper. One day the majority of my fish were caught like this. The only explanation I can give is that the perch fry may travel in small shoals, and that if the trolled flies travel through a shoal, there is likely to be more than one trout in the area.

97

On the drift: traditional-style fishing on Ireland's Lough Corrib

After this interlude, back to the dry fly. That is if 'dapping' can be called dry-fly fishing. Actually, it is probably drier than any other form of fishing, because not only is your fly dry, but so are the line and cast, which should touch the water as little as possible.

For those who have never dapped, here is the system. You need a 12ft or 13ft rod, a blow-line, a short length of nylon, a hook on which natural insects are impaled through the thorax (although artificial flies can be used as well), and above all a breeze. You raise your rod, let the breeze waft out the line and allow your dap to dance on the water. You should never drag it against the wave. Soon, if you are lucky, a trout will take it.

Dapping is another technique of fishing which seems to have

gained ground recently. From personal experience I know several lochs in Scotland where the dap was unknown before the war, but where many trout are now caught on it. To some extent it has replaced the wet fly, particularly for sea trout. The result has been heavier bags, which interestingly enough have not always been caused by a greater number of fish, but by the fact that a larger class of sea trout has taken the dap.

There are several interesting aspects of the dap. The first of these is the apparent difference between Irish and Scottish trout. As regards sea trout, the dap appears to be more successful in Scotland than in Ireland. Sea trout dapping is usually carried out with two large, fluffy, artificial flies, often black, one on the tail and one on the bob. Big sea trout, as I have said, are regularly caught like this, and salmon, too. But in Ireland, the wet fly still seems to work better.

With brown trout, the position is almost reversed. They are sometimes caught on the dap in Scotland, but far more so in Ireland. Dapping is the standard sport of many Irish fishermen. Only one fly is used, or rather two natural flies impaled on the same hook. The mayfly is used during its season, and later the daddy-long-legs. The method is far more successful than the wet fly, or the conventional dry fly. Here there may be a simple explanation in that the natural mayfly and daddy-long-legs are more common in Ireland than in Scotland, and the trout are more used to them.

Another really interesting thing about dapping is the strike. Here again there is a distinction between the artificial dap and the natural dap. When you fish an artificial dap, the trout will come up either with a head-and-tail rise or with a 'suck rise' from underneath. In the former case, I have usually been advised to strike as soon as the trout hits the fly. In the latter case, I have been advised to wait a second or two, and then tighten, but not to wait too long. In most instances, the advice has worked well.

But the Irish brown trout, rising to a natural dap, is quite another matter. If he does come up with a head-and-tail rise, you may be able to hook him by striking in the normal way, but this does not

99

often happen. Most of the trout I have encountered suck the flies down fairly gently. Sometimes all you see is a tiny, almost imperceptible ring on the surface of the water where the dap has vanished. Afterwards, you have to drop your rod-point, and wait, and control yourself, and wait and wait.

This is the biggest act of faith I know in trout fishing. Salmon-fishers, to whom a quick strike is often fatal, are well used to waiting. But a trout-fisherman, who knows that the trout has disappeared below the surface of the water with his flies, goes through agonies. If he strikes ('tightens' is a far better word) before a really slow count of about five, he is sure to lose his fish. His dap will come up again from the depths, sometimes with the natural flies stripped from the hooks.

If, however, he waits for about five seconds—a time that in his mind will seem more than long enough for a double-feature film programme—and then tightens gently, he will find that there is, almost unbelievably, a trout on the end of his line. He should not really 'strike' at all. Most of the trout-fishermen I have seen dapping for the first time have missed at least four or five fish before schooling themselves not to pull the dap out of the trout's mouth.

The best bit of advice I know for over-impetuous strikers is this: 'When you see a trout rise, take action—drop your rod-point'. At this moment of intense excitement, a fisherman always wants to do something. So long as he drops his rod-point, which in dapping is held high, instead of raising it, he will be all right. He will have time to collect his thoughts, make his count, and hook his fish.

November 1959   *Dermot Wilson*

A dilemma of reservoir trouting

The problem facing anglers on many reservoirs is whether to use a boat or whether to fish from the shore. This problem has to be resolved at the outset of a day's fishing or even earlier if boats are bookable in advance. The decision may have to be made many miles

The picket line: Northamptonshire's Pitsford Reservoir on opening day

from the water in question and sometimes before the angler has even
seen it.

The lure of boat-fishing is a powerful one, especially when we have
decided to spare neither expense nor effort to secure a brace of
takable fish. A boat gives access to 100 per cent of the water, whereas
the shore angler must content himself with perhaps a mere 5 per
cent. A boat may be drifted down to fish with the minimum of
effort.

Against these arguments in favour of boats it must be admitted
that reservoir trout like shallow water. Shallow water is warm, and
it is here that the flies hatch. Maximum weed-growth is here, too,
and nymph-type flies can be fished where they should be fished—
near the bottom. Other things being equal, most shallow water in
reservoirs is along the margins, and it can be reached easily by the
shore angler in waders.

All this makes as pretty a problem as you will find in fishing. Each

The new generation: still-water trout-fishers on the dam at Eyebrook Reservoir on the Leicestershire/Northamptonshire border . . .

season I have a great deal of amusement and interest in watching how different anglers react. At the reservoir I usually fish there is nearly always a couple of boats available on weekdays and the use of these is included in the ticket. Anglers arrive at the water in an agony of indecision. Should they row out quickly and try a few drifts first? Or would it be better to wade into a quiet weed-bed and work it over methodically for a couple of hours? Are the fish inshore or cruising? Is there a hatch on?

But this problem isn't always amusing. After a trip of 20 miles and

. . . and at Thames Water's Farmoor Reservoir, near Oxford

upwards people naturally want to put a hard-earned day off to its best use. Also, the price of tickets on the best reservoirs is substantial. A logical approach to this question of 'boat or shore' is necessary both for peace of mind and efficiency. No one wants to look back and realise that they have missed chances of fish.

First of all, it is wise to pay regard to the season. In spring the fish are invariably scattered and deep. Insect life in the shallow water is at a minimum. Only rarely will you see a rise and it is usually a waste of time to try to cover the fish. Fishing deep, in long parallel drifts from a boat, gives the angler, in such conditions, as good a chance as any.

When the weather warms up, shore angling is easily the best method. Fish which come into shallow water are almost invariably feeding. When they have fed they move out. This may seem a rather obvious observation, yet one often sees anglers fishing deep water from a boat when they should, in fact, be close inshore. Of course it is quite possible to drift shallow water in a boat, but unless one has a skilful boatman at the oars there is a tendency to over-shoot the fish.

On the whole—though there are lots of good exceptions—boats make for sloppy fishing. Tactics are often reduced to a mechanical 'chuck-and-chance-it'. Since the angler is continuously laying his flies on new water, there is a tendency for him to have his mind tuned one cast ahead. I don't think this is good fishing. It becomes too easy to miss a rise during the current cast. Moreover, there is a strong temptation when in a boat to cover as much water as possible in the energetic belief that it helps the bag. In my experience it seldom does.

One of the main virtues of shore-fishing is the fact that the angler can achieve maximum invisibility. A tall angler sitting in a boat is visible to the human eye for roughly half a mile. The same angler, wading in chest-waders and wearing a camouflaged jacket, would be inconspicuous at 50yd. There is no need to plunge into the vexed question of whether fish are boat-shy or not to see the force of the above illustration. Clearly it is better to give a trout as little to see as possible.

Before making a final decision about fishing a particular reservoir, the extent of the wadable margins should be ascertained. Some margins are not wadable; in other cases the reservoir banks are fenced or otherwise impassable. There is a tendency these days to construct reservoirs with steep sides, which rule out wading. Small reservoirs with popular-priced tickets tend to be overfished along the margins. On these, the boat-angler no doubt stands the best chance. On some waters boating is not permitted and the angler is left with no choice in the matter.

Having made a choice—boat or shore—it is best to have the strength of your convictions. An amusing instance comes to mind. Last season, while wading, I netted three nice trout within half an hour. Two of them became weeded and there was a certain amount of splashing before they found the bag. Presently an angler in a boat came over to watch. He tried a series of short drifts on my side of the water. Finally he moored the boat and began to fish from the shore some 50yd away. Neither of us had a fish after that, but it clearly showed up the indecision mentioned earlier.

March 1959   *F. W. Holiday*

Spring could be a little late this year

For brief moments I almost believe that spring has come. The sun shines warmly, casting encouraging shadows across the room. Horace, our large, grey-haired cat, winks a blue eye approvingly and settles in the most inviting patch. Just as I decide to drag out the sandpaper and brush up last season's rusty hooks, it starts to snow. As though a blind has been drawn, the sky darkens and my hand fumbles for the poker to stir up the fire. Horace glowers and stalks haughtily off, convinced I am responsible for the change in the weather. And that's the way it's been for weeks.

A few foolhardy souls have been out for salmon, but more as an act of defiance than a serious attempt to fish. However, spring must come, I suppose, sometime. Up here, at the top of Scotland, in Caithness, we have to wait a bit longer. Many anglers never consider an outing before the end of May. Even then a sudden snowstorm can leave you white, frozen, sodden and gasping. Consequently, March and April, to me, always seem the longest months of the longest part of the year.

As I write, snow hurtles past the window, driven by a force eight gale. Through the blizzard I catch an occasional glimpse of the Wick River cascading uncontrollably over the weir. Then, suddenly, the sun begins to shine again, the cat comes back and I fetch the fly-box.

Each year as the troutless months advance, the sense of excitement mounts. A warm anticipatory glow begins to fill the body—like Margaret Thatcher thinking of general elections or Red Rum approaching the penultimate Grand National fence. Do you have that same feeling? That fish will still be there, will still rise to the carefully presented fly, and will continue to do so at least until the end of the season? Do you have this sure and certain knowledge that all will be, eventually, well?

I must confess that it's the 'eventually' bit that bothers me. Not until that first fish is safely in the boat do I relax. It's surprising, also, how often the first fish comes from the same spot, to exactly the same fly, at exactly the same time each year.

Since we came to Caithness I have taken fish each season on our first outing to Loch Watten. At about 9pm just off the entrance to Lynegar Bay, I catch two fish, one immediately after the other. The first fish is always about $1\frac{1}{4}$lb, the second 1lb. The fly is always the same, a local pattern, the Ke-He, and the trout in magnificent condition.

When we lived in Northumberland, for five years the first catch was always below Hardriding, near Bardon Mill on April 23, across from the notice board on the Willimotswyke bank, to a size 16 March Brown and from $\frac{1}{2}$lb to $\frac{3}{4}$lb. I know it all sounds like the

Preparing for an early-season day on Loch Insh, Invernesshire

Hatched, Matched, Dispatched column of a daily paper, but it's true. Further back it was always on the Tweed, just up from Innerleithen on a stretch called the New Water. Early in April a small Greenwell used to do the trick.

I believe that fishermen, like fish, are creatures of habit. While this probably accounts for the repetitive nature of the first catch of the season, I can assure you it is a habit I have no intention of curbing— it's far too comforting and reassuring.

It's started snowing again, and the cat's attacking the fly-box. Time for more coal on the fire. Well, not too long to go, anyway. This year we (the family) propose to fish one new loch each month, as well as our old favourites, of course. This is an asset of the North that makes up in no small measure for the late start to the season. It would take several lifetimes to do justice to all the waters available; even those lochs within half an hour's drive will keep me going for years. Slightly further afield there are thousands of lochs in Sutherland at our disposal, not to mention Ross-shire.

In other ways, too, I am fortunate. You see all the family fish. The youngest finds casting a bit tiring at times and the blood-knot is still a mystery to her, but after all she is only two-and-a-half. Naturally, a great deal of family rivalry is engendered, and last year we decided to purchase a trophy. It is known as the Sandison Cup, and is awarded to the member of the family catching the largest trout during the season, fly only.

The addendum is for my wife's benefit. At the first hint of rain she can be seen digging for worms with an energy that would make Sir Derek Ezra, Chairman of the National Coal Board, green with envy and bring every pit in the country to an immediate standstill.

We also intend to begin a 'proper' fishing register, complete with maps, where X will mark, hopefully, the spots, and accurate, descriptive and informative passages concerning our local waters. For posterity, you understand. Just the thing to enliven long, dark evenings. Perhaps we'll start tonight!

It's nearly time for the weather forecast. I'm almost tempted to listen just to hear them explain away today's stop-start-snow-sun conditions. Still, it must have done a lot of good. Rivers will have been scoured clean, weeds drowned and our lochs will start the season full. There is something magical about a Highland spring.

In its clear, crisp days one senses the promise of long, warm evenings, midnight sun and the sound of water lapping the margins of the loch. It pre-empts the magnificent solitude of lonely hills, a soaring eagle and the happy sound of rising trout. Were it not for the dull, dank months of winter, these thoughts of pleasures to come would not exist. It must be meant that way.

However, when all is said and done I still have this date at the end of May just off Lynegar Bay on Loch Watten. I have no intention of being late and hope the trout feel the same way, so if you will excuse me, the cat and I must get on with the sandpaper and rusty flies. I'll let you know how we get on. In the meantime, 'tight lines' from us all.

March 1978   *Bruce Sandison*

These long, hot days of summer

Most of us have to plan our major fishing expeditions fairly well in advance. For this reason, and because of the fickleness of the British summer, we have to take pot luck on the weather; not only the weather in which we shall roast or freeze while fishing, but also that during the week or more before the trip, which will dictate the state of the water when we arrive.

Thus it was that, having arranged in May last year to spend a long week-end in pursuit of sea-trout on the Torridge in August, I grew increasingly despondent as blazing day followed blazing day through July. Those fish need rain to make them run, and not a drop had fallen for weeks. The heat-wave showed no signs of breaking as it ushered in August, and my spirits were low as I drove down to the West Country in what others might have described as glorious sunshine.

It has become a part of the ritual to hang over the old stone bridge below the village before driving on up the hill to the inn. On this occasion gloom hung around me like a shroud as I surveyed the river. The stickles, such as they were, made not a sound. The water, tinged with a thin, rust-coloured suspension, trickled idly between the stones. The pools, normally dark and polished, were low, and a thin film of creamy scum had formed wherever the current had totally died. And the sun beat down.

I drove up the hill, unloaded the car and started to erase the effects of the journey with a ploughman's lunch. The bar was busy. The door on to the square was open, the midday pint-pulling was in full swing, and all around was chatter. No, nobody had taken a peal for 10 days or more. Oh, yes, plenty were in the river, but they were torpid and stale. You'd see them from time to time, leaping clear of the water to get some oxygen across their gills, and crashing back again like a case of house bricks. Even the native brownies were difficult to move. I went up to my room and unpacked.

Five o'clock found me three or four miles from the village, walking along the tree-studded bank of my favourite beat, really for want of something better to do. However, there was a gentle breeze and, as the gradually sinking sun played its rays between the branches, my spirits rose a little. Surely things couldn't be all that bad? Surely a little careful thought might make the fishing worthwhile rather than just a duty?

I tried to assess the situation rationally. The peal were unlikely to provide anything more than purified frustration. Notoriously difficult to tempt at the best of times, in conditions like these they would be nigh impossible. The experts were unable to spur them into action, and I am anything but an expert. But the brownies were still there.

In the spring, these ferocious little fish, running at two and frequently three to the pound, are the most determined feeders I know. Now they were said to be tricky, and certainly few indeed were showing. In addition to my more robust sea-trout tackle, I had taken the precaution of packing a light $7\frac{1}{2}$ft brook rod and its accompanying bits and pieces. Could the weather which, until a few moments ago had seemed to be an all-embracing catastrophe, perhaps be turned to advantage?

Trout hate high temperatures and bright sunshine. They were likely, therefore, to be concentrated in deep water beneath shading trees, bushes and banks. Fish feed more readily when the water is well oxygenated than when it is not. Thus it seemed to follow that a deep, shaded pool, fed by a little running water, might contain a few feeding trout. I turned and walked a little more briskly towards the car.

Not far from the tail of the beat, close to the road, a stickle runs down from a long, smooth pool towards the side of the river's course. Its drop is a little steeper than the average and, even with the water as low as it now was, there was a soft splashing at its foot where it joined a deep, narrow run beneath the vertical bank. Further down, the river is open to the sky; here it is overhung by a huge oak whose branches stoop to within 3ft of the surface. When the river is swollen, this tree's branches are swept by the current. White, dried weed, hanging among the lower leaves like matted cobwebs bore witness to the spring floods.

As I approached the stickle, I heard a positive splash above the murmur of the running water. Keeping low on the bank, I peered beneath the overhanging boughs and watched as three pale, watery duns drifted from the upper pot. They were the first identifiable surface flies I had seen. I lost sight of two of them in the stickle. The third took a more sedate course, sailed out on to the run and slowed with the current. The trout rose through the shaded water like a cautiously surfacing submarine. He backed a little to keep pace with the fly, sipped it in without a sound and sank back into the darkness. A minute, irregular ripple spread and died.

Back at the car I put up the little rod and, having primed it with a 6 × leader and a small Tup's, returned to the old oak. Putting a fly on to the foot of the stickle so that it would drift naturally on to the glide was tricky. If anybody is short of Tup's there are probably two of mine still sitting in the branches of that tree. I gave the water a rest for a quarter of an hour after the first fish, smoking a cigarette and watching a kingfisher at work on the top pool, and then took another wild little brownie from exactly the same place as the first one. Then, with two more flies in the oak tree, a little intemperate language and one more fish, it was time to head back to the village in the dusk.

The following morning I was on the river at 5.30am. With no hatch of fly, and no rise apparent anywhere, I continued with the previous evening's train of thought. The water should have cooled overnight. The fish, if they were hungry at all, might have spread out from their deep and sheltered hollows in search of food. A small Greenwell's Spider is one of the best general imitations of a midge pupa that I know. Fished very slowly, just beneath the surface at the feet of the slightly faster-running stickles, it proved the thinking right. I had three more takable brownies by breakfast time.

During the morning, as the sun rose higher in the sky, the fish sank down and moved into the shade. If they were still prepared to feed at all, it had to be on something that lived on the bottom. Apart from my faithful old hat and a pair of wader socks, I could find nothing with which to collect samples from the river bed. Hot it may have been, but my plans did not extend to up-ending myself in mid-stream, and the shallow margins seemed to be singularly devoid of edible, animal minutiae.

But why should a deep, slow-moving pool on a river that had been low for weeks be so very different to the depths of one of our home counties' still-waters? Corixa? Corixa! Delving about in a fly-box, I found a somewhat battered imitation which, fished deep and slow in the stillest water beneath the trees, provided me with two more fish before the scaly siesta set in at 11.30am. After lunch I tied two or three more for use on the following morning.

The rest of the week-end was a delight. The pattern of the previous 24 hours was repeated with minor refinements and modifications. Those wild brownies, small as they were, provided far more than their share of excitement on the light tackle.

It was with sadness in my heart that I hung over the old stone bridge for a last look at the scarcely-moving stream and bade it

Trout-fishing at Blagdon, 'Queen' of the English reservoirs

farewell until the spring. Black clouds gathered as I drove away and, by the time I had gone 20 miles the windscreen wipers were earning their keep for the first time in weeks.

August 1976   *Peter Lapsley*

The Blagdon 'boil'

My grandfather saw it, my father saw it, and now, at long last, I have seen it for myself—the famous, or at least famous in our family, Blagdon 'boil'.

Blagdon is, of course, that trout lake, very beautiful and tree-lined and set in the hollow of the Mendip Hills, in Somerset. And legend

113

has it, derived from paternal and maternal grandfather, who fished it when it was a new raw reservoir 70 or 80 years ago, that there are certain times, just before dusk, when the trout at Blagdon go mad. They do not rise to the fly as normal trout do, with a dimple here and a dimple there across the lake. They do not feed on nymph or sedge in a normal decorous fashion, one at a time, with no rush or indecent haste, but congregate into huge shoals in some shallow bay and rise more or less simultaneously, violently. And for a very brief moment the whole surface of the water is churned with rising fish. This, says the family legend, is the famous Blagdon 'boil', when, according to my father, you could catch 'monsters of trout'.

It is pleasant, after a long period of time, to be able to say that the Blagdon 'boil' is not entirely fiction. There is much truth in the legend. And making allowances for much that is wonderful and awe-inspiring in the minds of fishermen, which is made more wonderful by the encrustations of time, nevertheless the 'boil' does happen. I have seen it.

I had fished there, at Blagdon, all afternoon with a high wind blowing down the gullies of the Mendips, tangling my flies, whipping huge tumbling waves across the lake, and not a fish had been seen. The late August afternoon dribbled away into discomfort. With lunatic optimism I went back there after dinner with only about half an hour of daylight left and with most of the other anglers on the lake packing up and going home. I was hoping to get just one fish before darkness came.

There was a boat out on the lake still, but no one else was in sight. There was no fly on the water, hardly a midge, but the wind had dropped. For the first time that day the water was still.

I fished from the bank, casting into a narrow sheltered bay where there is shallow water between banks of soft weed—Home Bay Point, I believe it is called. I used a rejoined 2 × cast and two flies, a large Invicta on the point and a slightly smaller and rather tatty Black Pennell on the bob. Why these flies? I do not know, except that I had been using them on a cast of three that afternoon and this was the remnant of a glorious tangle. But, for that matter, why not these flies? One choice, I reflected, seemed as good as another. The water was absolutely still, not a mark, not a ripple.

I shall have, I thought, rather good casting practice and, in any case, the lake is beautiful to watch.

Suddenly, in this still water, I saw one rise. It was 7 or 8yd out from the shallow edge in 3 or 4ft of water. Then there was another rise, and another, all more or less in the same area, in a kind of semi-circle in this narrow bay.

These were not the humping rises of trout, or the head-and-tail rises, and still less the gentle rises of trout poking their nebs above the surface to take fly on the film. These were great swirling turns. First of all would come a broad, curving back, apparently twisting round in the water, and then perhaps the flick of a tail. One, two . . . three, four. . . .

The rises became more frequent. I felt there must be fish all round me, and as I realised that I had my first trout—a very elegant, fighting rainbow of 1lb 6oz.

As I went back to the water after that and waded out a yard or so I knew I was in for something good. The rises were happening now almost simultaneously in three or four places. Again I had that strange feeling that fish were all round me. I could hear rather than see some of the swirls in the water, because of the semi-darkness. But that part of the water where there was still a glint of light seemed to be in turmoil, fish after fish breaking the surface, and nearly all, so it seemed to me, making that queer swirling turn.

I knew that something very odd was happening and my throat felt dry with excitement. A rise like this was bound to produce something very good.

It was just at that moment from the movement of light, the flicker of water, that the impression of boiling, bubbling water came into my mind, and I remembered out of the blue the family legend of the Blagdon 'boil'. It was an awe-inspiring moment, standing there on the edge of the darkening lake, the fish rising madly in front of me, and suddenly, as it were, my two grandfathers and my father standing inside me and saying inside my mind—this is the boil. And as this impression came to me I hit into a big fish. What with one thing and another I was awed and scared and trembling.

There was a huge bang on my rod, the line cut away through the water, the reel began screaming, yard after yard of line, and then the backing was torn off the drum. The power of that fish was terrific, boring out deep and downwards towards the centre of the dark lake. Somewhere out there, deep down, it finally stopped—for some reason of its own, I thought, because it had never seemed possible to me to stop a fish of that size. I had a few yards of backing left on my reel, and that was all. Even so, I never expected to get the fish in. There was too much power.

Inch by inch I wound in the line. The rod-top bowed even further, in a great arc. Slowly I strained back on the rod and put on full pressure. Inch by inch I pumped the fish in, and slowly, circling widely, it came in to within 20 or 30yd and then made a second run, enormously powerful, boring out deep. How many runs it made, I do not know, but they were several and they were long.

I shall never have any idea how long it lasted. I know my knees were trembling and my wrists were tired. I changed the rod from one hand to the other, letting the fish circle, using the full spring of the rod against it. The cork butt was close in to my body, the rod point pressed back hard right over the shoulder so that the big fish was fighting not only me but all the skills of all the craftsmen who had ever fashioned and worked in split-cane. Meanwhile, I cursed to myself, and aloud, reverently, at the size and the power of the fish.

At length it tired and came in and I walked back and beached it slowly on its side on springy-soft sedges on the edge of the shallow water. When I put my landing-net to the fish it was wider than the gape of the net. It was a big brown trout, beautifully marked, the size and shape of a young salmon, 20in long and weighing 3lb 8oz. It was a great moment.

Back on the sink of the farmhouse kitchen I discovered the cause of the Blagdon 'boil'. Both this fish and the smaller rainbow had their stomachs stuffed full of tiny minnows and rather larger sticklebacks. For those few moments of time in the late evening the big trout had come into the shallows to hunt the shoals of small fish. The peculiar turning, curving, rise in the water is, I believe, the trout turning round after its dash through the shoal to catch some small escaping minnow. That, at least, seems to be a reasonable explanation of the 'boil', which is certainly not like any other rise I have seen.

It was satisfying to prove that a family legend of 70 years or more was true; but in fishing one seems to prove something only at the expense of creating another mystery. Why should big trout, coming into the shallows to hunt minnows, madly chasing minnows as they were, allow themselves to snap at mere Invictas and Black Pennells—for neither of these flies could be said to look anything at all like a minnow? Were the trout in a mood to snap at anything which moved in the dark water, whether it gleamed silver or not?

But at least one can deduce from this the simple truth that when trout are on the feed they will even take flies, which is a comfort to the angler. And at Blagdon, when the 'boil' is seen, my father was undoubtedly right when he said you can catch 'monsters of trout'.

February 1964   *Conrad Voss Bark*

Learning by experience

I suppose that one of the first signs of old age is a tendency to look back into the past rather than forward to the future. My mind frequently reverts to incidents in my youth when I was learning to fish the hard way, by trial and error, with no one to guide me. One outing I shall never forget was my first visit to the Colne at Fairford. It was in May 1931, and the fish were just beginning to take an interest in mayfly.

About noon an old gentleman arrived, sat on his shooting-stick, put up his rod, placed a cast to soak and proceeded to have a

A big brown trout from Grafham Water. It weighed 9lb 7oz and was caught by John Matthews, of Oxford

leisurely lunch. I noticed, however, that he kept a close watch on the water in front of him.

Meanwhile, I was casting furiously at every rise both above and below him, but I knew enough not to disturb the water in front of the old boy. About 3 o'clock he put on his cast and fly and began to fish. He had a nice fish at the very first attempt. Another pause for a smoke and in about half an hour he started off again. He packed up about 5 o'clock with three beauties in his basket—and I was still without a fish.

The old fossil had hardly fished at all while I had worked hard all day. At the time it all seemed so very unfair. Just one fish would have meant so much to me in those days. I realise now that all I was doing was spreading alarm and despondency—alarm in the fish, despondency in myself.

One is so apt to forget that on clear, smooth water a thick fly-line scares many a fish between you and the one you are fishing for, and these in turn upset your particular fish.

I can recall many instances of catching trout by the exercise of observation rather than casting skill. One such concerned two large fish poised high in the water under an oak tree on the opposite bank.

Having failed to interest them with a selection of floating flies, but without having put them down, I lit my pipe and just watched. After a time it became obvious that their activities increased whenever there was a puff of wind and, looking up at the oak, I noticed that the young foliage was badly attacked by those funny little creatures that let themselves down on fine web.

I quickly cut off all the hackle from a green-bodied fly and cast it across to the fish. The result was immediate. Both fish made a lunge at it and, in my excitement, I struck too soon. After a pause to allow myself and the fish time to relax, I cast again, taking great care to be a little short of the nearer fish. It leisurely drifted across and sucked down the fly. Later in the day I removed the other trout with the same tactics. Ever since that time I have always kept a few green caterpillars tied up for use under oak trees in May and June.

On another occasion, when every trout in the river appeared to be rising to a fall of mayfly spinners, I worked myself into a fit of desperation by floating an assortment of spent gnats over their noses without any result. Eventually I gave up and crawled flat on my stomach to the edge of the river to watch more closely. I quickly discovered that for reasons best known to themselves, the fish were taking only flies that were completely spent and were ignoring any that showed the slightest flutter of life.

Wriggling back from the bank, I sucked my dry fly and flattened out the hackle. I was into a fish at the very first cast. Then another fish took immediately and I think I would have emptied the river had not a violent rainstorm put an end to everything.

I have since noticed that trout taking spinners appear to move about more than when taking duns. Perhaps they are better able to see an object that has penetrated the surface film. But whenever I see this happening and cannot see what the fish are taking, I try the 'sucked hackle' technique—and sometimes get results.

When I first went to Ireland to dap I had a very indifferent boatman and was disappointed with my lack of success. But on the third day I changed to an experienced boatman and immediately began to catch my share of fish.

It was not a question of knowing where to fish, but one of controlling the drift of the boat so that it travelled straight down-wind without slipping sideways. Both men controlled the drift with an oar on the windward side, but the first boatman did not fish and was therefore unable to see that the flies were continually being dragged sideways. With the second man, who fished at the same time, I noticed that my dap always appeared to remain in the same position relative to the rod. This was accomplished by frequent but gentle pulling or pushing of the oar. It made all the difference to this otherwise simple and at times rather boring way of fishing.

I think the most exciting fishing that I have ever had was when the wind dropped on these Irish lakes and there was a big fall of mayfly spinners. The great lake trout would then cruise along the surface with their tail and dorsal fins sticking out of the water, sucking down everything in their path.

Great accuracy was necessary when casting. I started off by chasing the fish, but soon found it quite impossible to strike properly due to the boat not being fitted with four-wheel brakes. This caused an enormous bow in the line immediately it was laid on the water, and it was not until I managed to curb my impatience and remain stationary until a 'cruiser' came in range that I began to get results.

December 1965   *Stanley Woodrow*

American trout

Trout and salmon are very similar. They are members of the family *Salmonidae* and are natives of the northern hemisphere only. In the Atlantic and Pacific oceans migratory salmon and trout have equally the same range—from Arctic regions to latitude 36° and 40° N.

In considering American trout it is over the word 'char' that our first difficulty arises. Char are distinguished from salmon and trout by the presence of teeth on the head of the vomer; in salmon and trout teeth are present on the body as well as the head of the vomer. Char prefer cold water; a temperature above 59°F is fatal to them. They are placed in the genus *Salvelinus*. This may seem easy, but in the United States several fish that should more accurately be described as 'char' are termed by the more general word 'trout'.

A long time ago, when the ice came across the parts of the world in which we now live—in the Pleistocene or Glacial age—the ancestors of salmon and trout came with it. They descended through the Atlantic Gap and the opening now known as the Bering Straits seeking a more congenial situation in preference to the long Arctic winter. When the ice retired and the weather became warmer, colonies of the immigrants which had become freshwater-dwellers were trapped in the streams in which they had made their homes. They have remained there ever since.

Relics of the Glacial epoch, isolated in their streams and developing different characteristics in the different environments, these fish, over the centuries, have been gently changing themselves into distinct species, and but for the interference of man they might have succeeded. In the first place, all the country now known as the United States was bisected as far as trout were concerned. The freshwaters that drained into the Atlantic were the home of the genus *Salvelinus* (the chars), while the Pacific seaboard was occupied by the genus *Salmo* (the trout). *Salmo clarkii* (the cut-throat) and *Salmo gairdnerii* (the rainbow) lived in all the streams flowing from the Sierras and the Rockies. These two fish in all their manifestations provide the majority of the fish known as American trout.

Today, however, it is impossible to state from the fish you put in your creel whether you are fishing in New Hampshire or Nevada. The barren lakes of the high West have been stocked with eastern brook trout (a freshwater char from Maine) and the rainbow from western streams has gone everywhere. The processes of evolution and adaptation have received a nasty setback. Trout formerly separated by impassable geographical barriers are now inextricably mixed.

That impressionable creature, the rainbow, has had a particularly rough time. An eastern brook trout or a Dolly Varden is much the same wherever it is found, but the rainbow, in all his glorious varieties—Kern River trout, McCloud River trout, Kamloops, golden, steelhead—is a problem.

The typical rainbow (*Salmo shasta*) from the McCloud River is a lovely fish. Bluish-green above, below silvery, profusely spotted all over, a red lateral band on each side, he reaches in the Sierras a length of 10 to 30in. *Salmo shasta* can be reasonably easily identified, but what of his relations? The brilliant little fish with golden sides (and even as an adult bearing the parr markings of an immature trout) that evolved in the Kern River, by Mount Whitney, is blood cousin to *shasta*!

What is a steelhead? Well, the adult steelhead is a trout that has spent part of its life in the ocean. He is a sea-going rainbow. Steelheads that reach maturity without leaving the streams are sometimes to be found in steelhead-dominated rivers among the migratory fish. These 'landlocked' steelheads are—rainbows.

To complicate further, the Kamloops, the dominant trout of the Canadian Pacific is a form of rainbow. The principal point of difference between them is in the number of scales (145 or so along lateral line for Kamloops, 135 for rainbow), but if the temperature be raised during the embryonic period, Kamloops can be produced with as few scales as the rainbow. The two fish are climatic variations of the same species.

Roy Eaton, editor of *Trout and Salmon*, with a brace of well-marked brown trout from a Scottish hill loch

Shall we return, for a moment, to the other representative of the genus *Salmo* from the western coast. *Salmo clarkii*—the parent form from which all other cut-throat trout have been derived—has not opened up such a vast field of diversities. *Salmo clarkii* is a silvery olivaceous fish, often dark-steel in colour, covered with round, dark spots. The inner edge of the mandible has the diagnostic mark—a deep red blotch. His underparts are a silvery-white and a pale pink wash is generally present on his sides. Varieties on the cut-throat pattern include a yellow-fin type, originally from Twin Lakes, Colorado, a fish with paler blotches on the jaw. The head may be a little more convex than usual. It is known as the Rio Grande trout. And a bluish fish with spots only on the caudal region is found in Idaho.

The cut-throat is a less spectacular fish than the rainbow; nor has he been transplanted all over the world. He is not migratory like the steelhead, but he will move out into tidal water, returning upstream whenever he feels so inclined and at no particular season. Cut-throats spawn in the spring.

Here, then, are the distinct species of trout native to America. The variations of environment, the whims of evolution, the corrective training of the hatchery man, and the transportations of the angler—these have played their part in changing rainbows to steelheads and Kamloops, the Columbia River cut-throats to the Yellowstones or Rio Grande cut-throats.

Now you will remember that in America trout and char are confused, so a word or two about the chars. The eastern brook trout (*Salvelinus fontinalis*) is perhaps the most popular. With the possible exception of the rainbow, the brook trout is the hardiest member of the *Salmonidae* in the United States. The back of this fish is more or less mottled or barred with dark-olive or black. He has a reddish belly.

The Dolly Varden (*Salvelinus malma*) is a slender fish, olivaceous, with large, rounded, red or orange spots on the sides and similar but small spots on the back.

The golden trout of Lake Sunapee (*Salvelinus aureolus*) originally native to New Hampshire assumes at spawning time a dazzling orange, with daffodil spots to his green shoulders. Two large lake trout (*Christivomer namaycush*) must also be added to the *Salmonidae* of the United States.

Altogether this is a group of fishes that offers many difficulties to the student of fish-life. He, however, feels amply repaid for his pains when he is confronted by such beauties as the moon rainbow (*Salmo seliniris*), or the golden char (*S. aureolus*) in all his mating glory.

February 1957   *Hubert J. Pepper*

III
Grayling

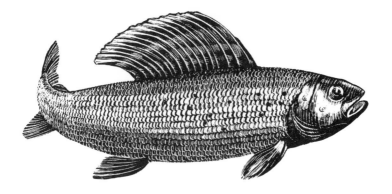

Grayling

Do grayling really have soft mouths?

I walked to the river under leaden skies, waders brushing harshly against the rough, coarse grasses of winter. The air was cold and the wind whipped across the open pasture. But any chill I felt was soon forgotten when I was close enough to the stream to see the distinctive plopping rise form of the grayling.

'Oh, those damned fish. No time for 'em!' I can hear some of you say. Well, that's as may be, but all I am going to say is that I am thankful that certain chalk-streams maintain controlled stocks of grayling to exercise my fly-rod throughout the fence months.

On this occasion I was fishing the East Riding chalk-stream controlled by the West Beck Preservation Society, and my host, Charles Derrick, secretary of the club, had, in the manner of the best hosts, left me to my own devices to make what I could of the day.

Fish were rising as I picked my way through the tussocks of coarse grass. The fly on the water appeared to be dark olives, which suggested a Rough Olive imitation, or something like it. Now I have long believed that the grayling can be just as selective in its feeding habits as the trout, and this I elected to put to the test.

What is the fly most recommended for grayling? The Red Tag, of course. I tied one to the 4× leader and cast to the fish. It floated over him without causing a flicker of interest. I continued the exercise.

I wonder why grayling are more difficult to put down than trout? Can it be defective eyesight in terms of long-range vision—that is, of the angler on the bank.

The Red Tag produced no take, so I reeled in and changed the fly for a Rough Olive. Now to put my theory to the test. The fly landed in the prescribed manner and I was rewarded with a convincing rise. A quick strike—most essential in grayling fishing, in my opinion—and the hook was home and a nice fish of 13in came to the net. This experience was repeated throughout the day.

Autumn glory: a good catch of grayling on bait from the Yorkshire Derwent . . .

I do not say the grayling is always as selective as the trout, but that there are times when it is, if not more so.

It is logical that as it takes the natural fly on the water as its normal diet, then a representation of the natural should bring success. On the other hand, there are times when it is possible to take the grayling on the Red Tag or practically any other fly.

Moving upstream, I came across another rising fish. This was an awkward cast, as he was feeding under the branches of an over-hanging tree. I managed to drop the fly—the same one, as the olives were still floating down—over him. He rose to it, but I was too late. My next cast was a shocker! The fly well deserved to become stuck in a branch, which it did. A search of the fly-box showed that I did not have another Rough Olive—a case of the cobbler always having the most badly repaired shoes in the village!

Back to the Red Tag I went, covering the fish a number of times. He wasn't interested. Sitting on the cold ground, I examined my meagre stock of flies. It would have to be an Olive Quill, a fly in which I have never had a lot of faith. Our friend under the tree found it to his liking nevertheless, and on the second cast took it. Score number two to the representational theory.

Feeling it was time to compare notes with Charles, I made my way back to the palatial fishing hut, reflecting as I went on the fortunes of grayling and how it seemed to have been neglected in so many angling books. Even passing references usually contain, to my mind, many inaccurate statements, the major one being that

... and a famous grayling fly: the John Storey

the fish has a soft mouth. Old Izaak, back in 1633, would seem to have started this off when he wrote '. . . yet he has so tender a mouth that he is oftener lost after an angler has hooked him, than any other fish'.

One cannot set too much store by the dear old fellow, as he went on to say that the grayling is pleasant to fish for in 'April and in May and in the hot months'. Well, that's certainly not so, as any experienced angler will soon tell you.

I have seen the soft-mouth theory so often in print, yet my own experience is that it just is not so. Not long ago I was casting to a trout on another small stream in East Yorkshire when the fly was taken by a grayling which eventually proved to weigh just 2lb. To land this, or any fish, was a problem, for between the bank and the water was a wide expanse of glutinous mud in which masses of reed were growing.

The problem was that the landing-net would not reach out to the fish, and to venture into the mud meant the certainty of sinking over the knees. Throwing old Izaak's dictum to the winds, I keel-hauled that fish through the mud and reeds. At the end of the performance the hook-shape had changed for the worse, but it had certainly not come adrift—indeed, its removal proved difficult.

This was not an isolated instance, and I have long considered that by and large it is easier to remove a hook from a trout than a grayling. Heresy? Well, as I said it is only my opinion based on experience. . . .

Charles now suggested that we walk together to the bottom boundary and then fish back upstream to end the day. He insisted that I move upstream ahead of him to have first cast to any likely fish. Grayling were still rising, but not with the same frequency as earlier in the day, and those I cast to I missed. I covered, and rose, one fish four times. Handing my rod to Charles, I suggested that he could catch it. He did, first chuck!

Nearing the hut, we stopped by a deep pool on the bend. Fish were certainly rising here. Creeping forward, I got within reasonable casting distance and dropped the Olive Quill over the nearest fish.

132

No response. Again I cast, with the same result. And again and again. Damn it, I'll try the Red Tag! First cast, up came the fish like a rocket. Why? I do not know, but I would have loved to have had an aneroid barometer by me at that moment!

November 1970   *Donald Overfield*

How big do grayling grow?

A very keen grayling fisherman of my youthful days used to think that there were two kinds of grayling in our rivers. He regarded the streamlined, greyhound variety that afforded him the best autumn sport to fly as quite distinct from the deep-set, hump-backed type intent on feeding on the bottom.

He was wrong, of course. All grayling are members of the same family—a family in which the younger generations are proportioned on streamier lines than their elders. Build is also influenced by the predominance or otherwise of strong, fast water, and in an even greater degree by the quantity and the quality of the food available.

In my experience the tendency with anglers is to underestimate the maximum growth-rate of grayling, and in saying this I do not exclude those with long years of fishing for the species behind them. It may be quite true that Walbran, Bazley, Blades and other grayling stalwarts could rarely tell of anything in excess of near two-pounders in seasonal hauls that topped the thousand mark. It is equally true that many keen trout fishermen have frequented the same and similar rivers without landing a two-pounder, yet no one rules out the possibility of connecting with trout in the 2 to 4lb class and occasionally in the 4 to 10lb bracket.

Since trout and grayling are not only of the same family, but also share the same preserves, it has seemed to me for a good many years now that there should not be a great deal of difference in their respective growth-rates, nor in the size attainable in individual fish fortunate enough to reach a ripe old-age.

When I expounded this belief to fellow-anglers keen on grayling fishing in the years between the two wars, the more knowledgeable were not slow to point out that from 1885 onwards no one had produced a heavier rod-caught specimen than the four-and-a-half-pounder caught by Dr Tom Sanctuary from the Wylye at Bemerton.

The best I could do then was to instance an earlier 5lb grayling recorded by Blacker as having been caught from the Severn below Shrewsbury by one Samuel Taylor. There was also a five-and-a-quarter-pounder found captive in a weir-trap on the Shropshire Camlet. I could have told, too, of the badly-decomposed remains of a 28in Ribble grayling found by a colleague in the margins of the Long Preston Deeps, and of another, not much less, from the same locality, which escaped as it was being brought to the waiting net.

Actually, we had to wait until 1949 before a duly-authenticated capture for top honours was reported. Sixty-four years is a long time for any freshwater fish to remain unassailed at the top of the tree, yet when it was toppled from its throne, the record weight was advanced by no less than 2lb 10oz. What was also surprising, and somewhat of a blow for the chalk-stream fraternity, was the fact that the 7lb 2oz grandfather grayling that J. Stewart landed in July 1949, came from a rain-fed river, the Melgum. [*This fish is now believed to have been a salmon kelt—Editor*]

The Melgum is a tributary of the Isla, which, in turn, is a tributary of the Tay. J. Stewart's whopper was a descendant of grayling first introduced to the Tay at Kenmore in 1880. Conditions there being not to their liking, the originals fell downstream to turn up the incoming Isla, where they flourished and established a line of grayling of a better-than-average size.

Last century, liberations also put grayling on the resident list in the Nith, Clyde, Tweed, Teviot and Annan, but with the locals the breed is not held in anything like the esteem afforded on this side of the Border. Where anglers are salmon and sea-trout minded, very often the grayling is as one with the unwanted chub stocks, with a status little better than vermin.

Though as keen as the next on salmon and sea-trout, the late

Dick Robinson had developed a love for grayling fishing on Yorkshire waters before he finally took up residence at Penpont to become a regular fisher of the Nith and the Cairn. He told of anglers hooking some very big Nith grayling when spinning a devon for salmon and sea-trout. The best he had seen landed was a five-and-a-half-pounder, but he had played and lost one that was heavier. He would not have been surprised to hear of the capture of an eight- or nine-pounder.

When I happened to mention these big Nith grayling to my old friend Norman Goodwin, of Earby, he told of an outing that very season when he had landed the grandfather of all grayling. Having spent the morning spinning for salmon, he decided to try them with the worm in a deep pool while he enjoyed his lunch. Lobworm followed lobworm on to the hook and up the cast until he had a final offering that would just have been nicely accommodated in a teacup.

Half-way through his sandwiches, tweakings attributed to eels developed into a full-blooded take. Having duly connected, the fighting tactics of the fish left him puzzled until a first view revealed the monster grayling.

Duly landed, the fish was spotted by a farmer acquaintance who stopped to exchange greetings on his round of inspection. Could he have it to boil up for his dogs? No objections having been raised, he departed from the scene with the grayling suspended from a gill-hold, and with a good deal more than the tail fin trailing on the ground.

In his day Norman did a great deal of fishing for grayling, and he has a profound knowledge of the species. Why he parted so readily with so outstanding a specimen without so much as even weighing it must ever be a matter for regret and surprise. It was only later, on his way home and pondering over the experiences of the day, that he realised how very big his grayling had been.

More than once since I have made myself a dummy grayling and carrying it in the manner adopted by the farmer concerned, have endeavoured to obtain some idea as to its possible length. Being very conservative, I cannot achieve the hold, dangle and trail under 30in.

In the matter of weight-for-length where grayling are concerned, the information available is unfortunately limited, but it does establish that length-for-length trout weigh the heavier of the two. At 17in the differences may be as much as 4oz, and growth thereafter would undoubtedly call for a more liberal allowance.

Two weight-for-length scales in my possession give the weight of a 30in trout as 11lb 9oz and 10lb 15oz respectively. If you take the latter as the yardstick, and err on the liberal side in your calculations, then for a grayling of like size a weight of at least 9lb is indicated. If you think I am being unduly optimistic, let me add that that would be about the weight of a 30in barbel, and the barbel is slimmer.

January 1963   *T. K. Wilson*

Grayling under scrutiny

If May, in the angler's calendar, truly belongs to the trout, then October just as surely is the month of the grayling, that much under-rated game-fish so prized by our Continental friends.

I doubt if one in twenty fly-fishermen in these islands pursues this species with the same keenness as he does the trout, and the percentage of those who have put their minds to studying grayling behaviour in detail is probably lower still. Yet the grayling is pre-eminently a fish of clear and rather cold waters, which makes such a study both possible and rewarding.

The grayling is a moody fish, much more so than is generally suspected. It is inclined to be slow to come on the feed in these autumn months if a sudden drop in night temperature occurs, or heavy rains discolour the water.

Like most creatures of mood it can also be most enthusiastic and co-operative, when so inclined, especially if care is taken to conceal one's presence and intentions, both from the main shoals and the rather jittery outliers.

By watching the behaviour of a small shoal of these fish it is possible to learn much of the character of the individual grayling which comprise it. There are the elders, probably some six years old, often rather dour and deep-lying, and calculated to require a deep-sunk and fairly bulky nymph to move them. There are the hare-brained younger fish, altogether more suicidal. These may take time and again, on or beneath the surface, even if a ham-fisted rod keeps missing them in the strike. Then there are the sullen members of the shoal, suspicious from previous experience, perhaps, which need skilful angling to take even at peak feeding time.

An unalarmed grayling, really on the feed, is a relatively easy fish to deceive and hook on some rivers. This certainly applies to Wiltshire grayling. In Hampshire, in my experience, the grayling of the Test and its tributaries are easier than those of the Itchen. Berkshire grayling can be really dour and, at their most sullen, really have to be earned.

On the Continent, mountain grayling can be fastidious to a degree which would astonish those who have not experienced their wiles. This explains why the grayling is rated so highly in the Jura, Central Europe and the Balkans.

Once well hooked, a grayling is less likely than a trout to come unstuck through such tricks as jumping or going to weed. They try both, but are much more fish of open water than the skulking trout. Only rarely do they seriously seek shelter under the weed when the angler makes firm contact. It may be accounted for by the fly-fisherman being on a high bank above them, or so my own observations suggest.

They take advantage of their big dorsal fins to otter about across the stream, often getting well below the angler before starting to do so. Then if the hook hold is not secure, they may make their escape. Such tactics on the part of the fish are generally easy to counter in the daylight, simply by keeping the downstream station, moving smartly to do so if necessary. When wading at night you must hang on and tire your fish before working it back up. Night fishing, however, is primarily a November enterprise, so I shall not dwell on it here.

Grayling, I think, have rather better sight than is usually conceded. They seem capable of turning down and away from a fly at the last possible moment if they suspect the artificial. With patience, it is sometimes possible to make one of these wise fish fall into error, after many casts, delicate enough not to cause any panic. Usually, if well rested and allowed to regain confidence by taking natural flies or nymphs, deception of the grayling with an artificial will prove easier.

A really educated grayling quickly recognises an approaching angler who gets too close. Such a fish makes a difficult chalk-stream trout seem relatively easy to deceive, and there is no better quarry on which to practise your fly-fisher's fieldcraft.

At this time of year the fly-life on the surface of a British grayling river is very diverse—sundry olives, autumn iron blues, pale wateries, blue-winged olives, and their various spinners, as well as sedge-flies, needle-flies, craneflies and the like. At no other time do grayling rise to the dry fly so freely, and some days this is the most effective method of catching them, especially in the first half of the month.

As October wears on, and fly thins out, the nymph comes more into play. This month, both dry fly and nymph should be regarded as complementary. Traditional grayling dry-fly patterns include the popular Tags and Bumbles. I am content to fish for October grayling with an Imperial, size 0, if the duns on the water are mostly small, or size 1 if the blue-winged olive predominates. I am not disputing the efficacy of the traditional patterns, but as the Imperial does the job as well, and probably better, I have no need of them.

Likewise, I do not suggest that other people should fish a simply-wired bare 0 or 1 hook as their sole nymph pattern. My own experience merely leaves me content to employ this modest artificial myself, until I hit on something better.

I remember a cold October day on the lower Wylye last year,

ending in the first and one of the only frosty sunsets of the whole back-end season. It was a good day for fly, but the grayling didn't move at all until after noon. Then the Imperial took fish, for a time. I went over to the bare hook and took the first 13 grayling I tried for. Number 14 of that batch took a little half-heartedly, and let go—and that was that for the fly-fisher, although bait-anglers enjoyed fair sport until the red sun went down.

A week later, in milder weather, the grayling on that reach were surface- or near-surface-feeding until well after dark. Fickle, yes, but not wholly unpredictable if you study them and do not prejudge them on the dubious hearsay of folklore.

October 1967   *Oliver Kite*

IV
Sea Trout

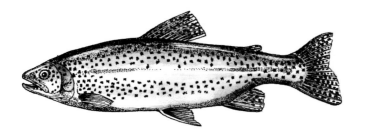

Sea Trout

Fishing in the autumn

Autumn, for me, is an angling season I can praise from my heart.

I write as a northerner, a Scotsman who has fished a good deal in the north mainland, and the far northern islands of his country. Autumn in such places means primarily sea trout. Sea trout, naturally, run earlier in the year in the south, and can run in the summer in the far north. Moreover, there are, of course, other angling joys, apart from those given by the sea trout in that part of the world in the autumn.

The big, late salmon is not, as is sometimes supposed, confined to the Tweed. I have even known isolated streams and occasional lochs in which by some freak of nature the brown trout were still in a condition in which it did not trouble one's conscience to take them in September. But these, let it be repeated, were freak places. I scarcely like even mentioning them, for, as every good brown trout angler knows, September is the month in which (however tempting the weather) one should be putting away one's brown trout tackle.

But the sea trout in the north in the autumn! There's a superb creature in the pink of condition and at the height of his powers. No conscience need prick one about dealing with him in the dying season of the year. He is as vigorous as the autumnal gales themselves and as full of body as the equinoctial tides and the autumn spates. The only trouble is nothing connected with rules, regulations or conscience, but the ability of being there and on the spot to deal with him. The far northern sea trout runs regularly in the autumn, but (alas for the angling holiday-maker with fixed dates to obey!) he chooses to run only when he is invited to by the spate. It is (and let us honestly face this fact) a matter of luck whether your autumn visit to the far north coincides with the sea trout's visit to freshwater.

I am, when I make these statements, thinking almost entirely about the islands of Shetland, where I have had the finest sea trout fishing I have enjoyed in British waters. I am thinking moreover of the peak days I have enjoyed there quite fortuitously when there happened to be a glorious run of these splendid creatures in August, September or even October when I happened to be there. I know, of course, that I was not particularly favoured by the gods. Anyone who visits these islands for a fortnight in mid-autumn is more likely than not to enjoy at least one run during his period of stay. Moreover, I know full well that even when they are not running they can be got in the voes (the estuaries) waiting to come up, and sometimes in the lochs or pools after they have come up.

However, since this brief essay is supposed to concentrate on the keenest joys of autumn fishing, let me confine myself for the rest of what I have to say to praise of the Shetland sea trout and just suppose that we are there when he is most plentiful and approachable.

The Shetlanders are unanimous in telling you that, pound for pound, their sea trout are stronger and more sporting than any other. They may or may not be right; but I who have felt their sea trout in the full blood of their vigour am not going to deny this patriotic island belief. On a day when the freshwaters are welcoming them in, and when the tide is beginning to flow, the sea trout come rushing up the voes and can be caught in salt water on sand-eels, lures of blue and silver, or indeed almost any gleaming object cast into their midst like a wet fly and then treated like a lure.

The actual casting does not demand much skill, though it does necessitate a strong arm. What does demand skill, or at least a clear head and the ability not to panic, is the treatment after hooking. In the flooding water of the incoming tide, with the intoxication of freshwater beginning to affect his blood, your voe sea trout does not hesitate. He either leaves you absolutely alone or takes your lure like a tiger. Often he will dart upon it from yards away so that you will see the quick wave of his approach before you feel him. The odds are then that if he takes you at all, he will take you well. You may as well just presume that he has done so; for if he is lightly hooked, not all your skill will hold him.

No, the skill consists in standing your ground and coping with him during his first mad rush to be succeeded by other rushes only slightly less mad. You must not panic when he takes you straight out to sea to a long length of your line, to conclude the run with a tremendous jump. It's easy to say that you must keep your head at such moments, but it is less easy to do so. The first run of an autumn sea trout in Shetland while still in the voe is so impetuous that it is apt to take your breath away. You just let him have his first runs to the ocean as he wills; for you know that he will of his own volition bring them to an end with the inevitable jump. The skill consists in just trusting to this fact and giving him his head, while always keeping the line sufficiently taut. That is until the moment of jumping, when, of course, you must ease off a bit.

There does come, however, an occasional moment when the skill of an instantaneous decision must be made. This is the dreadful moment when you realise that he has sighted a clump of seaweed and is determined to 'make it'. If (and it is important to make up your mind in a split second on this point) you are convinced that he is definitely making for the weed, you must, at all costs, put on all pressure. If he gains the weed, all is inevitably lost. If you put on all pressure, it is just possible that you may hold him or even deflect his purpose. But anything is better than the weed.

Southern anglers may say, and with justice, that such experiences and such decisions are not strange to them. I agree. But there is an intensity in the violence of an autumn sea trout's behaviour in Shetland which sharpens the edge of these experiences and decisions. You have to act more by intuition than by careful reason. And, to come as a surprise to you at the end of it all when you have got him in, he may turn out to be no more than 2lb. Is it conceivable that a two-pounder can have all this strength in his body, that he can have packed all this ferocity into one glorious fight? It is at such moments that you agree with the Shetlanders that there are no sea trout like theirs for strength.

Of course, there are sea trout many times heavier than 2lb in

Shetland. There are many other ways of catching them than in the voes when they are running to a flood. There are also many other joys to be found in autumn fishing for salmon and trout outside Shetland and in much more southern waters. The mere fact, however, of thinking about autumn fishing, of being asked to write about it tempted me as strongly as a blue-and-silver lure tempts a Shetland trout.

I leapt upon the pleasure of recalling and thinking of the few moments of intense, fearful joy in dealing with an urgent muscular sea trout in a Shetland voe to the exclusion of all other autumn fishing. I am sure that anyone who has shared my experience will forgive and understand. I have enjoyed many other forms of autumn angling and with bigger fish. But for sheer intense, exciting joy, give me a Shetland sea trout of 2 to 3lb, coming up with the flood tide during the autumn season. There is no fish quite like him.

September 1959   *Moray McLaren*

The temperamental sea trout

I don't think that anyone who has had much experience of sea trout would disagree with the statement that of all the species of fish which inhabit our rivers and lakes, they are the most capricious and temperamental.

Why, for example, are they so much shyer than salmon? Presumably, it is shyness which makes it necessary to fish for them after dark, or in coloured water by day. And to make the question more difficult, why is it that there are rivers and lakes where they will take freely in daylight as, for example, the Kildonan Lochs in South Uist, about which the late Major R. A. Chrystal wrote 40 years ago in his book *Angling Theories and Methods*?

While I have fished for salmon in upwards of 20 rivers in England and Ireland, practically the whole of my experience of sea trout is confined to one, the Tavy in South Devon. It is a typical moorland stream of the rocky, rapid type, which rises in the bleak uplands of

Fresh from the sea. . . . Two sea trout from Loch Voshimid on the Isle of Harris

Dartmoor and falls not far short of 2,000ft in a course of some 20 miles.

Another curious thing about sea trout is why there should be so few or none in some rivers while others within a few miles have plenty. The Tamar is a case in point. It shares a common estuary with the Tavy, yet I estimate that of the fish which come in, nine out of every ten salmon go up the former, while 19 out of 20 sea trout choose the latter.

Another interesting example is the Exe, which has even fewer sea trout than the Tamar although its mouth is cheek-by-jowl with the Teign and Dart to the west and the Axe to the east, all of which hold large numbers of migratory trout.

One thing I think one can say with certainty about sea trout is that the shorter the time they have been in fresh water, the easier they are to catch. When Lord Seaton lived at Buckland Abbey, he asked me to teach his gamekeeper to fish, and gave me permission to go to the Abbey water more or less when I pleased. I was thus in a good position to notice the big difference in the catches one could make there and in the association water above.

The Abbey water is the lowest beat from Denham Bridge into the tide at Lopwell, and so most of the fish in the pools are usually fairly fresh. The two best days I ever had there were 19 sea trout, and 18 sea trout and a grilse. Both of these bags were made by spinning a small devon in coloured water by day, and on both occasions I was meeting fish all the time I was on the water, and must have landed, lost, pricked, or seen come at the bait but turn away without touching it, at least 60 or 70 sea trout.

In the same conditions I have never caught more than six in the day in the association water from Denham Bridge up to Tavistock.

There are exceptions, but most of the big Tavy sea trout are not very pretty fish. Even when fresh-run they are not silvery, like salmon, but a sort of dull steel colour, thickly covered with black spots. The heads are short and blunt, quite different from the sharp nose of a salmon.

Probably more than 90 per cent of Tavy, and indeed all West Country sea trout, are caught at night, and their reactions to one's efforts are, in my experience, quite unpredictable. Sometimes one will meet fish at fairly regular intervals over a period of several hours. At other times the taking time may be no more than half an hour or less, while what seem perfect conditions of weather and water may result in a complete blank.

Probably the worst possible evening is one when, after a very hot day, such as one often experiences in August and September, there is a sharp drop in temperature after the sun has set. Then the cold air impinging on the warm surface of the water causes wreaths of mist to rise in what I call 'smoking water'.

A wild fish in a wild setting as Grace Oglesby plays a sea trout on Loch Voshimid
on the Isle of Harris

Sea trout are, I am sure, very susceptible to changes of
temperature, and I have often noticed that when a clear, starlit sky
clouds over and the air feels appreciably warmer, fish which have
been dour suddenly begin to take freely.

From sea trout in general I turn to one in particular which I
caught last season, because this fish was interesting in several ways
and unique in one.

I arrived at the river at 10am to find it a good height, but dark
with peat stain after a big flood the previous day. This black water,
with great bergs of foam on it, is never very promising, and I was not

surprised that I fished for two hours with only one half-hearted knock from a sea trout. Then about noon I noticed that the water was turning cloudy. By 12.30pm it was the colour of yellow ochre, probably field-washings from a storm somewhere upstream.

This is what I call perfect peal water, for, as long as there is no weed coming down to foul one's hook, it can hardly be too dirty for sea trout. My hopes ran high. Yet for half an hour I never had a touch. It was exactly one o'clock, and I was just thinking of knocking off for a bite of lunch, when I had the hard strike so typical of sea trout.

The next five minutes were quite unique in my experience. The speed of the first run was fantastic even for a fish which often makes a fast first run. Then the line went slack and I thought it had gone, and there was only about 5yd of line out when I felt it again. The moment the line tightened on the next three occasions the same thing happened. To try to stop such rushes would have been disastrous.

Each run ended in the same way with the line going completely slack and I wound in feverishly, completely ignorant as to whether or not the fish was still on. Of the five minutes for which the fight lasted, I am sure I was not in actual contact with the fish for more than about 60 seconds. It is the only fish I ever landed in which the rod played practically no part in the fight.

The end was almost as dramatic as the beginning, for its last rush back on a slack line left it stranded half out of the water within 5yd of where I stood. It lay there quite motionless while I reeled in the slack. When I was in contact again I walked forward and picked up without a protesting kick a sea trout of exactly 6lb.

I started again and with the third cast hooked and landed another of 1½lb. And that was the end, for although I continued for another hour in what appeared precisely identical conditions, I never had another touch. The actual taking time was no more than 15 minutes in the two hours of perfect water.

January 1967   *Kenneth Dawson*

Dappers' delight: a good wave on Loch Maree, the famed sea-trout loch of Wester Ross

Sea trout from salt water

Three summer holidays of fishing for sea trout in a Highland sea loch is a short enough experience to justify dogmatism. But a lifetime of trout fishing in freshwater has taught me to beware of illogical positivism. Here, however, are a few observations on salt-water sea trout which might be of interest to any angler who would like to try this fishing.

I assumed at first that, since sea trout have to enter a sea loch to reach the rivers that feed them, the narrows would be the likeliest places. Perhaps so, but, if so, my tactics were wrong. Instead, wherever there was a rocky, weedy shore, shallow enough for wading, that was where I had most success.

My experience with boat-fishing has been limited and not very rewarding. I read somewhere that the shadow of a boat in salt water can be mistaken by the fish for that of their greatest enemy, the seal. If so, they behave very differently from ordinary sea fish, which have no fear of boats. I like wading because it helps me to search and linger among the rocks and weeds. Sea trout can be caught in open water beyond the knotted wrack, but I get more in the awkward places where it would be difficult to manoeuvre a boat.

At first I cursed the seals and their inquisitive investigation of my fishing activity. I imagined a stampede of fish away from their threatening presence, until one day, I caught a two-pounder within 30yd of a whiskered face.

I remembered how I once watched a cat stalk a singing thrush in an apple tree. The thrush hopped to a higher twig with every step upwards by the cat. It never stopped singing. Wild things are wary of their enemies, but seem to feel little fear of them except, perhaps, in the moment of capture. I fancy the sea trout behave like the thrush. Life goes on much as usual in the presence of danger.

Spinning in salt water can be successful. Spoons and the like are quite good, but terribly vulnerable among the wrack. The slightest error of casting, or failure to commence an immediate retrieve, leaves you hooked up. A 12lb line is an almost necessary insurance. It allows you to pull most entanglements free without loss. But it reduces sport.

Spoons that revolve round a central barrel are easier to manipulate in the difficult places, and the vibration probably helps. Small lures seem better than large lures. Of the colours, I like silver and gold, and green or blue touches are good. I have a small pot of blue paint with which I obliterate any red markings. Why red is good in freshwater and almost useless in the salt, I don't know. I am almost dogmatic on this point. And fast retrieve seems better than the slower method of the freshwater fisher.

A certain guide-book says that Loch Etive is the only salt water where sea trout can be taken on the fly. This is nonsense. I've watched land insects, blown on to a sea loch, snapped up by the trout. But most of the flies I use are not insect representations, as far as I know. Almost any attractor loch-fly may succeed, especially those with silver or 'Lurex' bodies. But I'm rather conservative. More experiment might make other discoveries. I prefer fly-fishing to any other method. I can fish more accurately, more delicately. I get hung up less often and can scale down my nylon to about 7lb bs. Losses are less expensive and the fun is more furious. When the tide is out, I can cast beyond the jungle of weed and use even finer end-tackle.

In salt-water fishing, the question of questions must be—what state of tide? The last hour or so of the ebb or the beginning of the flood are possibly the best taking periods. Most of my catches, however, have been made in the later afternoon or evening. One or two forays in the early morning and towards dusk have not been encouraging. Sea trout do not seem to behave like other sea fish, and I have not caught any after dark, which is surprising. My best river-fishing for sea trout keeps me out of bed for hours.

My first and third sea trout holidays were continuous heat-waves. In 1967, I had a month of never-ending rain and storm. In the heat-waves, the hotter the day, the better the fishing—always on condition of at least a little wind. Calm conditions seem as difficult as on freshwater lochs.

Catches, of course, will vary from loch to loch. My biggest fish was less than 3lb. I'm happy with a few pounders and sometimes have to be content with the smaller finnock. I seldom fish for more than two hours and am lucky to catch three or four.

Sometimes I return only with stories. A common one is about inquisitive fish that follow the fly or spoon right to the rod-tip and then shy away. That can be exasperating. To lose fish because of hooks blunted or broken on the ubiquitous snags is quite a frequent occurrence for which only one person is to blame.

And we all know the corrosive effect of salt water and should take appropriate precautions.

February 1969   *C. R. Pearce*

V
Salmon

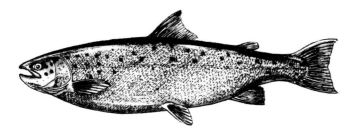

Salmon

When the river turns sour

Like many other mature, responsible and quite sober men, I cannot resist staring longingly at any river—even more longingly, perhaps, at those I have no hope of fishing than at those in which there are prospects. I would unhesitatingly choose 10 minutes relaxed viewing of, say, the Test in preference to a spin round the finest of cathedrals or an afternoon in a gallery filled with old masters.

Going to Torquay this last spring, the train gave me a sensational railside tour of the Exe, roaring by beat after beat and pool after pool. It was bank-high and brown (the Americans would have called it 'riley'), but my appetite was wetted by imagining the life under the surface—trout easing into the calmer backwaters, kelts backing hopefully towards Exeter and, perhaps, a spring-newcomer.

If the rivers were empty, I might not spare them a glance. The charm of watching them depends on the possibility of seeing the underwater flash of silver or the quick movement of a dark shape. But for this, I might spend more time with the flying buttresses.

Between seasons, I am also haunted by a series of fishing dreams, or nightmares, that are really not the sort of dreams a responsible, mature and quite sober person should have to endure. Their invariable theme is one of gloom and frustration. The rivers are empty—sometimes waterless rocky beds—or so flooded that they can be seen only from far-off high ground, or filled with oily, stagnant and quite unfishable water. As any psychiatrist would quickly diagnose, such dreams are merely the mirrors of the sad days beside out-of-order rivers that are the lot of those who have to accept the hopeless odds of holiday-only fishing.

All this night-and-day dreaming serves only to build up the excitement when the time for the real thing arrives. Even before I set out, I will have been enjoying vicarious advance pleasures as the rods, boots, bags, reels and nets are inspected, double-tested and heaped in the time-honoured corner of the hall. Why it all has to be piled in this particular corner is something that those in command of the house's law and order keep asking—but how else is wholesome tradition created?

Excitement increases steadily through the journey, during the instant inspection of the river (low, but not, surely, absolutely hopeless), during the night and through the hastily-eaten and untasted early breakfast, hitting its peak when, rod up, fly tied with trembling hands, packed lunch stowed away in the fishing hut, the first tremendous steps are taken into the water and the fishing begins.

Although on the previous evening the river had seemed to be low, once in it, with the current pressing the backs of the waders, it becomes clear that there is plenty of good water left. And if from the heights of the town bridge it had looked unhealthily clear, it seems now to have just a shade of desirable colour in it—by no means ideal but certainly beyond expectation. Perhaps during the cloudless and starlit night, a freshening shower had confounded a logic in the far-off mountains. . . .

What is totally unexpected, though, is the skittering upstream wind that concentrates itself around the top rings of the 13ft rod, so that although the line is curling out in fairly acceptable fashion, the 9ft of nylon and fly are alighting gently upstream of and at right-angles to the line. No salmon has ever taken a passing lure which is preceded by a formidable curve of thick, dressed plastic.

The grip on the rod is tightened and a little more punch is put into the next cast. The fly is straighter, but a splash in the water behind (only 9in from the trees on the bank) is a reminder that something horrible happened to the back-cast. Next time, the line flies back high and true—then remains fully extended, fly embedded in the branches of a bush.

Out of the water then (no need to wind in, just coil the line in long loops between reel and first ring), undo the fly, wade in and start casting. But by now the coiled loops are round both waders, nestling snugly underneath the useless straps that encircle each instep. With

158

a sigh, I do what I should have done in the first place—wind the lot in and start again methodically.

Gradually the casting begins to defeat the wind. The water for the first time is covered properly. Wrists are aching a little and there is the smallest sensation of lumbago round the pit of the back, but at least the fly is being presented in an adequate way.

Two hours have now passed. The time is five-to-eleven. I ask myself, suddenly, 'What fish?', realising with resignation that not one salmon has shown, and that I have already covered two of the finest holding pools on the beat. The sun breaks through and the water gleams, clear as crystal. The gravel at my feet seems to shine. I notice a layer of slime at the water's edge, an unwashed look that makes me wonder how many months ago there was any extra water. I also start to nourish the suspicion that there is not a fish within miles.

That, of course, would have been the moment to leave the water, sit on the bank, relax, sniff the air, watch the wagtails and the dippers, listen and purr. In every other sport there is a half-time interval or tea-break, but not apparently in the game played by a fishing fool. All he does is stand in the water, take off the promising fly, put on another far bigger or far smaller—and start heaving away again as though a second's delay might lose the opportunity of a lifetime.

It takes two further hours to fish down to the final legitimate yards of the beat and put a few casts for luck into the water just beyond. By then the feet are leaden, the back is frozen into an ugly curve, the wrists and fingers are aching, and something is sucking and splashing inside the waders. The river, so fresh and lively at first has suddenly turned sour.

And that is what it is all about. After the long, slow drag back to the fishing hut, after the bottle of beer and the sandwiches, as energy begins to return, there by the rock on the other bank—no doubt about it at all—a smooth brown back dips porpoise-like in the run, right over the taking place. All of a sudden the river looks great again, teeming with promise. Adrenalin racing, hand showing a satisfactory tremble, tiredness gone, back into the water I go with all the enthusiasm that might be expected from a mature, responsible and no longer quite sober man.

July 1972   *David Barr*

Springers in the snow

I have never liked cold weather, yet every spring I brave frost and snow to fish for spring salmon, and I wouldn't miss those early outings for anything. Last spring, for instance, there were several days when it froze all day and the trees looked as if they had snow on them, with every twig whitened. Lines kept freezing and fingers had no feeling in them. Yet I loved every minute and enjoyed a fine feeling of satisfaction when the day was over and we swopped tales by a roaring fire.

Spring fish are surely the finest fish of the year, straight from the sea in their silver and pigeon-blue. And spring fishing, where the angler has to fight the elements, is more of a challenge than the later fishing, and after the extra endeavour one senses that feeling of well-being that follows the completion of a difficult job.

I remember a spring day on the Tay when snow lay all around and a frost persisted throughout the daylight hours. I trekked about a mile from the hut to my favourite pool, carrying two rods and a bag, and wearing waterproofs and waders. I hooked a fish when I started and sledged it ashore over the fringe of ice along the edge of the pool. When I picked that fish up later from the snow, it was as stiff as if it had been in a deep-freeze. During that day I had another three fish.

When I went to pack up I decided to make a sack of sorts from my waterproof jacket. Then, with the fish wrapped in the jacket, and the rest of my gear gripped as well as possible, I set off for the hut. After I had struggled along for about five minutes, one of the fish slipped out of the jacket and fell on the snow. Before I had time to do anything the other fish followed. Laboriously I packed them again and started off.

The load seemed to grow heavier and heavier and I was glad to glimpse the hut some 200yd away as I rounded the corner of a wood. Just then the fish quietly slid to the snow once more. This time I did not pick them up, I simply threw my jacket beside them and went on.

My host and the two gillies were at the hut and I asked one of the gillies if he would take some basses and collect the fish. He asked what size the fish were and I told him that when I left the top pool they were about 14lb each, but when I dropped them they were about 56lb each.

I will always remember the first spring salmon I caught. As a boy I was given the occasional day on a stretch of river near my home. On arriving at the river on one such day, I was dismayed to see a man fishing down the other side of the pool I was to fish. I knew he was poaching, but since I had been quite friendly with him in the past I did not like to question his right to be fishing. I watched him from among some river-side trees and was nearly reduced to tears when he waded right into the salmon lie I had intended to fish. In the shelter of the trees I put up my rod while he fished. Then suddenly, to my delight, he came out of the water and hurried off downstream.

When he went out of sight round a bend, I went down to the pool. I was convinced that I would have no hope of a fish until the place had settled, but decided to begin the cast. At the third cast, and in the lie from which the man had waded only five minutes previously, a salmon took my fly. It was a lively, fresh-run twenty-two-pounder.

Salmon are not easily scared, although when I am fishing for them I go about it as though they were as shy as trout. That fish had obviously been driven from its lie by the wading man and had returned in a state of unrest when he had gone. Perhaps without the disturbance I would never have caught it.

Often on bitter spring days I think about the theory that salmon will not take a surface fly when the air is colder than the water. This is not always the case, and I have had many fish which took a surface fly in such conditions. Once, when fishing on a Donegal lough, a

Spring on the Wye, and a salmon-fisher tries the tail of a pool at Erwood, below
Builth Wells

bitter wind with snow in it had the temperature down to about freezing point. I said to my companion that if a fish was mad enough to take, it would do so under the surface because of the cold air. No sooner had I said that than a salmon came violently at my dropper fly as it was on the surface at the end of my retrieve. The fish was more than half out of the water as it took. Next day the same thing happened again.

When snow is on the river banks and snow clouds are overhead, so that the water looks almost black, I have found spring fish to take well despite the temperature. I have always believed that the light has much to do with the taking or non-taking times of salmon. Dark lights are good, and so is sunshine from a cloud-flecked sky. It is when the sun comes from a cloudless blue and the water has a hard, metallic look that my hopes dwindle.

So, while I write this in the close season, I have already looked out my spring tackle. And along with it are lying gloves, scarves, wool lining for my waterproof coat, and heavy stockings for inside my waders. I love my spring salmon fishing—but no, not the cold!

February 1971   *Ian Wood*

Reflections on catching a salmon

The catching of a salmon, or indeed of any fish, may be likened to a drama in three acts, the hooking, the playing and the landing. In the first the fish can be said to play the leading part. It has the initiative since, except in a case of foul-hooking, unless and until it collaborates by seizing the fly or bait the drama can hardly be said to have started. The angler's initial moves in presenting his lure can be considered as no more than the overture. Some overtures, like some orchestras, are better than others; but they are only the prelude to the more important things to come.

In the second act the roles are of equal importance, and like jealous actors each strives to impose his will upon the other and steal the show. In the case of the angler this is, of course, deliberate, but

163

Dejection: Eric Horsfall Turner and his boatman ponder their next move as Tweed, thick with 'grue', shows one of its less welcome moods

how far is this true of the efforts of the fish to escape, and by this I mean are its actions dictated by anything approaching reason, or simply by fright at having its movements restricted by what is probably the terrifying tension of the line?

I am a confirmed sceptic that the fish can reason to the extent attributed to them by some people. How often one reads in fishing books and articles that the fish deliberately tried to rub out the hook on a rock, or, with malice aforethought, ran round the far side of a snag to foul the line.

One writer even made the astonishing statement that every fish hooked in a certain pool immediately ran through a large rock with a hole in it with the deliberate intention of breaking line or cast. That, surely, presupposes that every salmon, as soon as it arrives in a pool where it means to stay for a while, makes a careful reconnaissance of the layout, and notes every feature likely to be of use to it in time of trouble. In other words, the fish expects to be hooked!

Surely if it can reason to this extent it would also have enough sense to resolve before coming into the river to avoid the temptation of snatching at the tantalising objects which hover and dart around and about its lie? It does not want to eat them anyway. From the human point of view the story seems just as improbable.

If anyone really had such a pool, which never yielded a salmon, although obviously a good lie, surely he would do something about it? I know I would, for a stick of dynamite is all that would be necessary to shatter the rock and remove the hazard. After all no one really likes losing fish and tackle.

I wonder how many people really enjoy playing a salmon, and by this I mean that the whole thing is sheer unadulterated bliss and undiluted happiness? I have fished for more years than I care to count, and have killed quite a number of salmon, although not, of course, anything to compare with the records of many people whose lines have always been cast on waters of the first class, such as the Wye, the Aberdeenshire Dee and others, where in any relatively good year their bag is counted by the hundred.

But even now, particularly at the beginning of a new season, my knees start knocking and my heart thumping when I feel the first heavy plunge of a hooked fish. And all the time I am playing it my emotions are excitement mixed with acute fear that I shall lose it, because when one fishes for the most part 'hard' waters, where a salmon is a salmon, and not by any means an everyday prize, one realises how true is the French proverb: *Partir; c'est mourir un peu.*

In *Thoughts on Angling*, J. C. Mottram, who is, I think, after Chaytor, my favourite angling author, describes the catching of a trout of 5lb 2oz on an Olive Nymph. He ends by saying: 'I did not really enjoy playing that fish, all the time fearing the 4 × gut'.

Personally, the only time I can really enjoy playing a salmon is if I don't care much whether I lose it or not. One has this feeling with a vigorous late-spawner or a kelt, and some of either category put up fights better than many a clean fish. I can agree with Chaytor in welcoming a kelt on the first day of a new season when, as he says: 'A pull of any kind gives you a jump of pleasure'. But one has to confess that such pleasure is somewhat insipid, and when the feeling of fear is removed the result is rather like an egg without salt or gin lacking bitters, while the sense of intense exaltation which follows the playing and landing of a right 'un is completely lacking.

I sometimes wonder if I should retain my keenness to the same degree if I habitually fished waters of the first class, where double-figure catches are nothing to write home about at times. A few years ago rods on a famous beat of the Blackwater averaged 14 fish a day each for a week or more. Similar catches are made in some springs on the Tweed, and on the famous Ridge Pool of the Moy at Ballina in Co Mayo. The late A. H. E. Wood said that he once hooked 41 salmon in a day at Cairnton, when the fish were really feeding on a big hatch of march browns, and he could not keep his fly out of their mouths. In 22 years at Cairnton he himself landed 3,490 salmon, and in 1915 he had 121 in 13 consecutive days. A lost fish cannot matter very much at times like those, and one could probably really enjoy the playing of them. But does one become blasé? I am never likely to know from personal experience!

As an omnivorous reader of fishing literature I am sometimes surprised at the views expressed by the authors; so often they conflict with what my own experience has taught me. Not long ago a writer advocated the playing of a fish downstream whenever possible because, he said, it was unable to breathe so well in that position. I know this is a widely-held belief, but is there any foundation for it?

Watch fish of any species cruising about in a pool, and it will be seen that they swim just as often, just as easily, downstream as up. Tens of thousands of kelts swim many miles downstream every spring, and it is only in dropping back over weirs or falls, or in very fast rough water that they keep head to stream so as not to be swept away out of control. Elsewhere they swim in a normal manner head in the direction they are going.

Elation: Tony Cherry, of Ringwood, with a 38lb salmon taken on the Hampshire
Avon at Avon Tyrrell

A fish being pulled downstream at about the same pace as the stream is taking nothing whatever out of itself; whereas when it is fighting both the force of the water and the strain from the line it is using up the maximum amount of energy. Years ago I had an interesting illustration of the difference. I hooked in quick succession two salmon in the tail of the same pool in heavy water. The first weighed 17lb and was on the bank in seven minutes because it fought upstream in the raging torrent at the head of the pool the whole time and when it came back to where I was standing it was completely beaten. The second weighed 9lb. The moment it felt the hook it bolted downstream and was gaffed 20 minutes later more than 200yd below.

In my experience the fish which persists in going downstream is the hardest to kill, and unless one is using very heavy gear, the one most likely to break you. In this case the double strain of fish and water is against the angler. I once heard that a man hooked nine fish in one day on the Awe; every one bolted downstream and broke him.

Richard Waddington says in his book, *Salmon Fishing*, that it is quicker to tail than to gaff a salmon. His actual words are: 'I find that I save several minutes of playing time with every fish'.

Now to tail a fish by hand in my experience means that you have to bring it into quite shallow water, and no fish I have ever played will allow this until it is too tired to resist. The last salmon I landed in 1955 was an object lesson in the superiority and speed of the gaff. It was in October when no gaffing is allowed, and, anyway, I did not want to kill it as it was a well-coloured hen of about 12lb.

It put up quite an exceptional fight for the time of year, running both fast and far, and it was 19 minutes before it could be tailed. Three times, however, it had come within range of a gaff, but on each occasion as its belly touched the shingle it dashed off again with renewed vigour. That salmon would have been on the bank in six minutes with the help of a gaff.

May 1956   *Kenneth Dawson*

A sparkle on the Spey as a lady salmon-fisher casts a fly over the Sluggan at Castle
Grant

Twirling for salmon

Thirty years ago when the method of greased-line fishing as evolved by A. H. E. Wood was first described in book form, many fly anglers, by adopting the floating line, considerably increased the number of the fish they killed on rivers during the late-spring and summer months.

About the same period Crossfield described in an article published in Farlow's catalogue the very successful method he used to catch salmon on flies as the spring water-levels of rivers began to drop. Crossfield's method differed from Wood's in that, instead of the fly being kept high in the water by the buoyancy of the greased line, it was kept near the surface because the ungreased fly-line was pulled in fairly rapidly as it drifted down and across the current.

During the past 20 years or so many angling writers have pointed out that when fishing with a greased line the most likely time to raise a salmon is just after the fly starts to drag. It is obvious, however, that the fly must drag, albeit slightly, during most of its journey across and down the river in spite of how often the line is mended or how expertly the fly is led. From the time it lands in the water until it ends its journey below the angler, the fly has been drawn either across the current or held against it by the line. The speed at which it drags varies. It is perhaps least just after the line has been mended, and greatest just before and while it is being mended, unless, of course, it has been mended in order to cause drag deliberately.

It was J. L. McMonigal, of Ballina, who has killed more salmon and grilse than most anglers, who first pointed out the advantage of having a large and well-greased knot on the end of the fly-line. By watching the knot the angler can easily see how fast it is dragging, and can arrange that during most of its passage across stream it makes a discernible 'V' ripple on the surface.

After adopting this method of continuous drag I noticeably increased the number of fish I caught each summer season in medium-paced and slow-flowing water. In slow-flowing water it is

Spring salmon-fishing on the Welsh Dee—the Fairy River—near Llangollen

usually advisable to aid the movement of the fly by using Crossfield's technique of pulling in line by hand.

It may well be, however, that salmon take the greased-line fly fished in the orthodox method for reasons other than the speed at which it drags. Possibly when the floating line begins to pull the fly, the sudden acceleration of the fly induces an interested fish to seize it. Or perhaps it is that as the fly changes direction from drifting more or less downstream to being pulled across-stream it becomes more attractive.

Once, when fishing the Ash Tree Pool on the Moy from a cott in July, I found that the grilse were unusually difficult to hook. Because of the nearly glass-calm surface, and the background reflection of high trees which overhung the river, it was possible to see some distance into the water. Plenty of fish were seen following the fly (there was a fair current), but they would not touch it; when the fly was pulled more rapidly they merely swam higher in the water and some showed their backfins or tail above the surface behind the fly. The nearest they came to taking the fly (a short-dressed Shrimp Fly on a single number 10 hook) was as it changed direction from being drawn more or less across the current to turning upstream, while the line, which was being retrieved by hand, straightened out below the boat.

To make the change of direction more abrupt a different method was tried. A line of about 15yd was cast upstream and across, but no more across than about 30 degrees. As the line drifted downstream the rod-point was moved down with it. By the time the rod was pointing obliquely downstream the portion of the line on the water near the rod-top was beginning to pull. The rod was then lifted and swung or gently cast directly upstream again. This action lifted half or more of the line and laid it on the surface so that it made a narrow 'V' with the tail half of the line.

As this 'V' drifted downstream, apex first, the rod was again moved in unison with it and was stopped at about the 45 degree angle downstream. The line then began to pull as the 'V' started to

On the Spey—and a good salmon comes to net on the Tulchan water

'unwind'. As the line forming the nearer arm of the 'V' lengthened, the other arm shortened, and when there was only a yard or so of line left on this other arm I began pulling line in by hand to increase the speed of the fly.

The change in the behaviour of the fish was immediate. Within the next hour five grilse and one red 15lb spring fish were in the boat. Not only did this method, which a friend of mine calls 'fishing the twirl', save the situation that afternoon, but since then it has accounted for many fish, when they have been reluctant to take a fly fished in the normal manner.

When this method is used the fly has time to sink several feet because of the distance the line drifts with little drag, and when the end of the line and cast are finally pulled round the apex of the 'V', the fly following the cast is drawn towards the surface. It may be that this ascending half-spiral-like course of the fly excites the salmon's curiosity.

March 1958   *J. R. Harris*

The gamble of the spate river

As soon as I realised that every office molehill had become a mountain and that my partners were beginning to loathe me, I prescribed myself a four-day break and took off for Scotland, packing a few fishing clothes, a rod, a reel, some nylon and twenty salmon and sea trout flies in a box.

I spent the night in Edinburgh, and was wakened at 4.30am by the rain lashing the windows. I was out of bed, dressed and away in seconds less than any known record, realising that if this rain was falling on the Deveron I might have very few hours of fishing indeed.

I reached Huntly by nine and called on Tom. Anyone who visits the Deveron, having that privilege, and fails to make this essential call, does so at his own risk. In between running British Railways and propping up the local telephone exchange, Tom contrives to catch fish under almost any conditions in almost limitless numbers. From him come freely the latest hints on dealing with the current river situation. This time he was not sanguine. There were fish, but they were dour. Another 3in of water were badly needed. Even so, it was worth having a go.

On then to Rothiemay. My arrival at my usual hotel was like coming home. While they were greeting me like a long-lost friend, busy hands were already putting together, unasked, the packed lunch and handing over the keys to the hut. Within half an hour I was parking my car under the trees on top of the brae, looking down on the ribbon of river below, recognising familiar rocks and bends.

It took two hours of hard casting, I suppose, to dull the edge of the

174

The start of the day as salmon-fishers set out from Kenmore to fish Loch Tay

first shining optimism, to take in the fact that, apart from smutting trout, there was no movement in the river. Unlike the great fishermen, I find that my casting suffers badly from a nine-month lay-off, and poor timing and back casts caught in thistles on the bank had done nothing to improve my morale.

After covering nearly a mile I remembered that I had had no breakfast. I returned to the hut and set about the packed lunch and two cans of beer. It was 3.30pm when I woke up. Another man was fishing for trout in the pool below me. The sky was cloudless, the sun was hot and I was lightly cooked on one side. I decided to return to the hotel and try again in the evening.

Back again down the brae at 9.30pm. The warmth had gone

and there was an unmistakable whiff of frost in the air. The light was still dazzling and not a salmon, not a sea trout, moved. Across the water, at Tachore, the opposition was firmly in charge, bag empty. I fished for two hours with little hope, and the mist came off the river like steam from a giant saucepan. Later, at the hotel, the trout fisherman joined me. His dry flies (mist or no mist) had caught him a dozen good trout. He told me that he had only just missed stepping on me as I lay asleep in the grass.

The next day, my last, was cloudy and soft. A little drizzle had made the roads wet without offering the faintest prospect of fresh water in the river. I fished with hope until lunchtime, casting technique in the slot again, no trouble with the bank, covering everything necessary. I was using a well-tried combination, Hairy Mary and Dunkeld in size 10, yet, though I knew it could not be improved upon, I was already suffering the temptations of that small voice that twitters in moments of failure, 'Why not try something bigger?'

Any taking fish would have reacted to my pair (as I knew from many happy occasions in past years) and I managed to resist the temptation to change my line of attack. Nor did I have so much as a pluck.

That evening after supper, Tom managed to arrange a stand-in at the telephones and we went down the brae again, in search of sea trout. By this time I was quite certain that the fish had all passed through in the small flood of a week before (one of the classic salmon-fishing myths we all adhere to when fish are not showing or taking). Tom assured me that every pool held fish, though not perhaps in great quantities.

We started fishing at 10.30pm in perfect night-fishing conditions. The best pool yielded nothing. We moved downstream. By this time it was after midnight, the northern night growing quite dark. I was fishing the choicest runs, with Tom following me or casting into places with which I had not bothered. At a quarter to one he hooked and landed a four-pounder that had been lying quietly in a shallow

176

glide. Ten minutes later, I felt two quiet taps and thought I had cast into the opposite bank again. There was a big mid-stream splash as I tried to jerk free. And that was it—my only take!

This, of course, is salmon and sea trout fishing. It is unpredictable, chancy, a ten-to-one-against gamble for those of us who fish the spate rivers at times chosen in advance. Altogether, I fished for 24 hours and travelled a thousand miles to do it. Yet, curiously, it was well worthwhile.

The rewards are not by any means necessarily the fish, and range from the first realisation of the change into Highland light (it happens around Stonehaven), through meetings with old friends and on to the sights and sounds of hill and river, the whistles of the oyster-catchers, the feeling of gravel shifting beneath the feet, the pressure on waders of clear, rushing water, and the eternal hope that the next cast will be productive.

The end result is unarguable. Back at work again, the molehills have resumed their normal tiny size.

October 1968   *David Barr*

When I go fishing

Whenever I see a river my first thought is: 'What kind of a place is this to fish in?'

No matter whether I am bent on business or some other pursuit, whether the stream be fleetingly seen from the window of a railway coach, or whether I am strolling along its banks. Should the stream be very small I can picture myself reduced in stature to fit it, and the tiny rivulet will have runs and pools which can be populated with tiny fish for which a projected miniature of myself may angle. Such day-dreams are rather good fun in which to indulge, especially as they are all anticipatory.

When I go fishing my mind is looking forward to what lies ahead. True, if the water is familiar, past incidents and experiences may come to mind, but both past triumphs and disasters have not the

A big, cold river for Air Commodore Douglas Iron fishing the Wye below Hay in
early spring . . .

same power of diversion that the hopes of the next few hours may
give me.

Should I have a companion who has experience of the water
about to be fished, I cross-examine him in some detail. But if the
positions be reversed I try, without becoming too garrulous, to give
him or her, a word picture of what to do, where to go, and what to
expect.

On arrival at the bank where operations are to begin, I find it
pleasurable to devote a few moments to contemplation. This is often
mistaken by those who do not know me well as being a tactical
reconnaissance on how the water should be fished, or how the fish

when hooked should be landed. In fact it is no such thing. My mind is merely indulging in a pleasant day-dream out of which I extract an illusory pleasure.

Most of the fishing I do is for salmon or sea trout. Both these species of fish are unsophisticated in that they are not so accustomed to seeing anglers' lures as are the non-migratory species. They come fresh from the sea, and though they may get a bit stale at the back-end of the season, they are usually prepared to make some sort of offer at some time. Of the two, the big sea trout is the more cunning. Indeed, on sober reflection, and when I am away from the river bank, I think the salmon is really rather a stupid fish, but his bulk and strength, aided by the water he inhabits, makes him a worthy opponent once he is hooked.

In the waters where I catch most of my fish, the rivers are free of snags in the shape of roots and fallen trees because these rivers flow beyond that imaginary line 'the northern limit of trees'. However, these waters are studded with sharp rocks in the form of lava and possess razor-edged corners against which no cast, however strong or sound, is secure, so that I am tormented by the fear that not only does a fish know where they are, but that he also knows what service they may be to him in his extremity. Of course the fish has no such idea in his head, and it is only after the contest is over that I realise how stupid my fears have been, or how unlucky I have been should, by blind chance, the fish have escaped from me because of one of them.

We read in the books on modern salmon-fishing how the angler with consummate skill, and using a greased line, floats his fly to the fish, and how the fish comes to view, rises, turns and takes the fly. Meanwhile, the angler, exercising stoical control, does nothing. Now I sometimes use a greased line when salmon-fishing, but (dare I confess it?) I do not suppose I see one fish in six that I rise, and I still seem to catch quite a few of them. My first intimation of an offer is usually the feel of the pull on the line.

Often I think that perhaps I am missing something that other and

179

. . . and a bright 15-pounder from the same water later in the season

more skilled anglers enjoy—but I wonder. I remember asking an old and very skilled angler what he considered was the best moment in salmon-fishing. I had expected the reply to be the sight of the rise or the first pull of the fish. But no, he looked at me for a moment and with a smile said: 'When you get back to the hut with three fish and no one else has any'. I still think he was pulling my leg, a thing he has done for many years.

I believe that to become a good angler a certain degree of concentration is necessary, but once the art of casting the fly is thoroughly mastered, a part of the mind can be allowed to wander. Except in the most difficult places, the purely mechanical action of placing the fly where it is required, and its subsequent control, can be left to a sort of instinct which all true anglers possess. The registration by the eye of a spot lower down where a fish has been seen to rise or show itself, can be noted without becoming unduly inattentive to the way your fly is fishing. There is, however, a danger in this process in that the lie, or even the pool, just ahead, looks a bit more attractive than the bit of water you are then fishing, and this is hurried over or neglected. I often find I have to use restraint when thus tempted and to force myself to advance at a steady rate of progress.

Again, at the beginning of a day's fishing, when an approach is made to a well-known lie, almost a feeling of dread possesses me as I approach the fatal spot. That swirl below the sunken rock is almost certain to house a taking fish, and as the fly approaches it the suspense becomes almost unendurable. How often have anglers' chances been thrown away by this rise in emotional sentiment?

Fishing is an emotional pastime, but we all of us carry an antidote—the spring balance, that soulless piece of ironmongery which delights in telling something less than the truth. But strange as it may seem, even spring balances may in the end develop a soul. I have had one in my bag for some 50 years. Its spring is softening, due to rust and long usage, it is no longer quite sure where the zero mark is, and its little brass pointer hovers somewhat below that symbol even when unencumbered with a fish. And when one of my younger companions says, 'Shall I try it on the kitchen scales?' My reply is a somewhat terse, 'Certainly not!'

January 1956   *Major-General R. N. Stewart*

The luck of the game

There is not the slightest doubt that luck plays an infinitely greater part in fishing than in any other field sport. And of all the many forms of the gentle art, none is more subject to the frowns and favours of the fickle goddess than is salmon-fishing.

I killed my first salmon at the age of six, and it weighed 19lb. This highly improbable story is true, but not so remarkable as it sounds. At that time the family was living in Suffolk and sometimes we went to stay with my grandmother in Bournemouth. One day, my father took me to watch the salmon nets working at the mouth of the Avon at Christchurch.

After a haul I asked one of the men what one of the fish weighed. He said it was 19lb. Then, for some unknown reason, he handed me the heavy, wooden priest and showed me how to give it the *coup de grâce*.

The second one I killed, after a lapse of about 15 years, came about in an even more improbable manner. By that time we had moved to Devon, and I had started to fish the Tavy as a complete beginner. I had had some success with trout, but none at all with salmon, for the occasional one I had hooked invariably came unstuck.

It happened in June of my third season that I was tying a fly on Tames weir-pool, not far above Denham Bridge. Halfway down I saw a salmon, lying belly-up close to the bank, and thinking it was dead and would be better out of the water, I gaffed it. Imagine my surprise and consternation when it started to lash about. My immediate thought was that if anybody had seen me I should be accused of snatching and so lose my association ticket.

However, the foul deed was done and the fish was on the bank.

The cause of its discomfiture was a flight of big trebles far back in the gullet. I heard later that the retired Admiral who fished the opposite bank had been broken by a fish two days before. He said it was a very big one, but actually it weighed only 10lb.

The biggest salmon I have ever killed in the Tavy weighed 23lb and took me one and a half hours to land. It was hooked in one of the fast runs in a very rocky stretch above a long, shallow pool. At first I thought I was on the bottom, as several hard pulls produced no response. Then the 'bottom' moved, and I saw a very big fish for the river swim past me. I noted that it was hooked in the front end of the dorsal fin.

After a 20-minute fight the 9lb line parted with a crack. But soon I saw a gleam of hope. The fish was lying quite near by the bank and about 15 yards of line were attached to it. Hastily I tied on another bait and flight and began dragging for the line. The first time I picked it up it slipped off the hook before I could get a hold, but the next attempt was successful.

Fingers all thumbs with excitement, I cut off the other devon and tied the two ends of the line together. When I tightened, the fish was still on.

The salmon shot down into the big, shallow pool and away under the far bank, from which long branches hung out over the river. To avoid getting the line hung up in these, I, too, had to take to the water. For more than an hour I slipped and staggered up and down the pool on water-worn stones as slippery as ice.

At last, however, the fish came to rest on the far side of a rock several yards out from my bank. I crept up stealthily and peered over the top. There was my quarry, lying in about 2ft of water.

Inch by inch the gaff went down until the point was well below the fish. A pull upwards was followed by tremendous splashing which soaked what little of me was still dry. Somehow I managed to get my violently struggling prize on to the bank. That was one fish I really felt I had earned, in spite of the way it had been hooked.

It is well known in the West Country that the pixies of Dartmoor

183

have complete control over the salmon in the Dart, and I believe that the leprechauns are the overlords of the salmon in Ireland, and woe betide anyone who offends the little people. Like their English cousins, they can be very malevolent. Offence I somehow must have caused all unwittingly.

On my first visit to Ireland, in 1939, all, at first, went well. I had a very good day on the famous Ridge Pool of the Moy at Ballina, killing six salmon and losing several others. But, after that, everything went wrong.

I was staying on the nearby Easky in Co Sligo, which was extremely low, and on the only two good fishing days in my fortnight, I was completely incapacitated by a badly swollen ankle. This could only have been the work of the leprechauns, for I went to bed feeling perfectly normal and woke up with the ankle swollen like a balloon and intensely painful.

And so the vengeful little people plagued me on every subsequent visit. True, I killed quite a number of salmon, but things happened to me over there which never happened anywhere else. For example, on one trip to the Slaney, I lost a salmon after gaffing it owing to slipping on wet rock. The bank on another pool gave way and deposited me head first into 5ft of cold water. Then I lost the biggest salmon I have ever hooked after playing it for an hour.

On the Suir in 1949 I was taking a photograph of Ballycarron Bridge with the camera on a tripod when a violent gust of wind sent it crashing to the ground. I could see no damage. But something had happened and not one of the photographs I took after that was any good.

Then, on the Caragh in Co Kerry, I lost a fish in the most extraordinary way. I hooked it at the head of the Boat Pool, which is more like a lake than a pool in a not very big river. The moment it felt the hook that fish came charging straight to me where I was standing on the bank and landed, after a flying leap, at my feet. Then, without a moment's pause, it shot off again and there was a crack like a pistol shot. I knew my line had broken, but when I looked I

Early-season harling on the Church Pool of the Tay, near Strathtay

saw that the top 6in of the light split-cane rod had been cut off as cleanly as though with a knife.

What had happened, I feel sure, was that when the fish jumped, with yards of slack line, the inevitable gale, which invariably followed me round Ireland, twisted a couple or more turns round the top of the rod. I have had this happen many times when my bait was snagged near the bank and then came free with a jerk. But has anyone else ever had a rod broken in this way?

I think the biggest stroke of luck I have ever had while fishing occurred on the Tavy in February 1951. Looking for salmon on this river in February is like searching for the proverbial needle in the

Matting the catch after a good day on Scotland's famous River Oykel

haystack. I could not get out until after lunch, and then found that the association water had been thronged all day, although no one had had anything but kelts.

A friend was fishing the Big Pool at Virtuous Lady Mine and when he had finished I went in at the head. Almost at once I was into a fish which proved to be a sixteen-pounder. I was about to leave the pool when the friend, who was sitting on the bank having a smoke, called out: 'Go on, get another'.

As no one else was in sight, I started again, and right across under the far bank, with almost the last cast, the incredible happened. I hooked another fish. This one fought like a tired fish, and had probably just recently come into the pool, for it was covered in sea-lice. It weighed half a pound more than the first.

April 1966   *Kenneth Dawson*

Salmon or trout?

My friend Oliver Kite defines the dedicated trout-angler as a man who will go anywhere at Christmas for salmon shooting. As a professional conservator, both of trout and salmon, I am bound to regard this as the indictable misdemeanour of incitement to commit a crime, for crime it is to throw or discharge any missile into any water for the purpose of taking or killing any salmon (or trout, for that matter).

Oliver, so far as I know, has never shot a salmon in his life. But when I came, years ago, to work in the South of England, I was flabbergasted at the information, freely proffered by a landowner of unimpeachable eminence, that his neighbour's head-keeper had the previous day shot a spawning salmon in the headwaters of one of our more famous chalk-streams. In the mountain fastnesses of northern England, where I was born, rumours had filtered through that salmon were not welcome in the metropolitan trout-fishing district of Hampshire and Wiltshire, but I had no idea that this was a serious matter.

Nor is it a straightforward one. In Scotland, trout have long received less statutory protection than salmon, and while, if you sought the latter on the Lord's Day you were headed straight for the Sheriff's Court, you could set forth on a Sunday morning, trout rod in hand, and risk nothing more painful than a wigging from the Minister. The Dee, if it flowed through Hertfordshire or Middlesex, would command astronomical rentals for its trout fishing, but many an Aberdeenshire laird will tab you 'never invite again' if you waste good salmon-fishing time casting for the brown trout which guzzle march browns on a spring day.

Can both be right? Are salmon vermin on chalk-streams? Are trout vermin on a salmon river? If not, where lies the truth?

The Caledonian war on trout is probably the less justified. Its protagonists claim that trout eat salmon eggs and oust the parr in competition for food. The work of Jones and King leaves little doubt that salmon eggs, well-buried in the redd, are nearly inviolable, and the ova with which, each spawning season, the trout are stuffed to overflowing are almost entirely those which scored an 'outer' on the redd pocket when ejected by the hen salmon. These eggs may represent no more than 5 per cent of the total discharged. They are, in any case, a write-off, for if the trout did not get them, nor the bullheads, eels, loach, dippers or caddis grubs, they would hardly survive the buffeting of their downstream jaunt.

Competition for food, or the all-important 'territory' essential for the growth of young *Salmonidae*, may be more important. But it is worth remembering that salmon make over 99 per cent of their growth in what the late Theodore Houghton, of Ribble fame, used to call 'the unlimited common of grazing in the sea'. Thus, provided it can acquire the few ounces of food necessary to bring it to smolt-hood, every parr stands an equal chance of providing the river with an adult salmon. Moreover, anti-trout campaigns are likely to be effective only if waged *à outrance*, and the imagination boggles at the prospect of de-trouting the Dee or Spey.

Attempts to rid the chalk-streams of salmon merit more serious consideration. Large fish spawning in the water-meadows are easy prey for the salmophobe, while it is an easy matter, by manipulating hatches, to hinder their migration and deny them access to the river upstream. What, then, is the case for the prosecution?

It is said that salmon overcut and destroy trout redds; that they compete with trout for food (a slightly amended echo of the Scottish charge); that salmon parr greedily take dry flies aimed at trout; and that kelts eat trout. Formidable indictments. But are they true?

The overcutting charge will hardly stand up. Experience shows that salmon habitually spawn in gravel of golf-ball size. Trout, on the other hand, simply cannot 'cut' such large gravel and lay their eggs among pea-sized pebbles, often in places where salmon cannot, or will not, go. The trout spawning season, too, is often a month later than that of salmon. Frank Sawyer, whose opinions on chalk-stream trout I would back against most others, has recorded trout spawning in March, while the salmon, even on the Frome and Avon, are mostly spent by Christmas.

Competition for food? If I live to be a hundred I doubt if I will see the day when the supply of fish-food organisms in the Wylye, Ebble, Anton or Candover Brook comes within a mile of over-exploitation.

Nor am I much impressed by the trout angler who complains that he is pestered by salmon parr snatching his fly. This frequently happens to northern anglers who search the whole river with a cast of wet flies, but the essence of chalk-stream fishing is to locate and identify a sizeable trout and then cast to it. It really requires little experience to diagnose the rise of such a fish or to distinguish it from that of a baby salmon.

Do kelts eat trout? I expect they do, poor hungry creatures. But when you remember that, at most, about 15 per cent of salmon (usually a good deal less) survive spawning, it can be calculated that in a normal year there may be no more than about 150 kelts in a small river system and then only for a matter of weeks. This is no more than the pike population in one mile of badly-kept trout water.

The final nail, I conceive, in the coffin of the case against salmon is to be found in the list of acknowledged salmon rivers which also provide good trout fishing—Lune, Eden, Don, Deveron and Welsh Dee, to name but a few. And I believe that the day when it can truthfully be said that all other trout predators are under control will be time enough to start setting the clock back and go forth to harry the salmon.

Thus far we have merely considered the proposition that trout and salmon cannot exist side by side. But this really evades the hard core of the problem. Does either transcend the other in desirability? How good must a trout fishery be to justify the exclusion of salmon therefrom?

I remember being appalled years ago, when considering the fish-passes on quite a good northern salmon river, to be told that salmon were not wanted upstream because they would ruin the trout fishing. I said then, and I believe now, that no moorland trout fishing is good enough to merit the hindrance of salmon from miles of good spawning ground. There are trout streams so excellent that their preservation would take precedence over the needs of salmon, but they can be counted on one's fingers.

An old Avon fishery-owner once said to me: 'Is it sensible to convert good trout water to mediocre salmon-fishing?' This is a fair question, and although I say again that the premise on which it stands (namely that we are bound to have salmon or trout) is ill-founded, it lies at the bottom of all controversy on the subject.

At this point I ought to make my own position clear. From time to time in the past, I have been accused of being a salmon-only man who sought to grow salmon at the expense of trout. I am not. I am a professional fishery conservator concerned only to put to the best use the waters with which I have to deal. And it seems to me common-sense to afford trout-fishery owners the chance of a salmon if this can be done by such simple expedients as levelling an obsolete weir or installing a fish-pass. The issue is bedevilled by fear of rating authorities or landlords. Tenants (some of whom have reached the limit on what they can spend) often fear that the advent of salmon will price their water beyond their means.

While I sympathise with this attitude, its logical conclusion would be the deterioration of British fisheries to the point where they were worthless to rating authority, landlord and tenant alike. In this day and age, when fishing is fast acquiring a scarcity value, it seems to me imperative that anglers should seek to divest themselves of labels and consider quite objectively the facts of the case. If they conclude, as I believe they must, that salmon and trout can live together, no effort should be spared to produce the maximum crop of both. We can no longer tackle the job of fishery conservation with the brakes on.

August 1965   *J. D. Brayshaw*

The frustrations of salmon fishing

The wise will say that frustrations in fishing are unnecessary; that they can be avoided by the simple application of the fruits of experience. Don't go to the river when the pools are low; don't go until fish are running; don't waste time when they are obviously ploughing on with no intention of being intercepted; change the fly for a spinner; try a sprat.

The wise, of course, have skill and extra-sensory perception. They never get their eye wiped by the newcomer who stands back and waits or the chap they allow to go down first, fishing exactly the same fly tied to the same size of hook in what appears to be precisely the same manner. They are experts to a man. If they have red-letter days they land 10 fish. If they have blank days it is because they sniffed the wind and stayed at home when lesser individuals flogged the water to a froth and swore to give it all up.

Very well, it isn't luck. It is skill and experience. I bow to the skilled and the experienced. They have all lived longer than I have or they have lived more intensely. I dare not whisper that they have missed just as many fish and blundered as often on average. They would be upon me at once. Let me say that I prefer to be frustrated with a trout rod in my hand than trying to outdo the heron at the pools, but that is my particular kink. I don't see my madness as a dry fly fisherman, but I see the undoubted obsession of the salmon angler. I see it and feel the horror that a man who loves his glass feels when he encounters an addict.

What takes a salmon? If we are to believe all those who have made serious contribution to the literature of salmon angling, the fish that does/doesn't feed in fresh water takes almost anything from a flaccid sort of lure that looks like a bunch of bananas to a rat or kitten's tail, spinner, wobbler, clothes peg, rag, bone and hank of hair. It takes the small trout-fly and the great monster-fly that was once fashionable on the far northern salmon rivers when rods were 18ft and more in length. It takes worms in bunches and the highly skilled fish-of-the-week chap, who keeps coming back to the salver in the hall casually to tell admirers that he had one half as big again in the same month last year, will smile a superior smile and shrug his shoulders when I tell him that boys dangling all kinds of baits in the salt water have hooked good salmon. They have landed them, too, because estuary and sea-anglers have to use tackle fit to take a fish out of the tide-rip.

Two summers ago I went north to the haunts of my boyhood to fish as good a river as ever a salmon ascended, a place as entirely free of ticket anglers as any river could be. For company I had my son and we devoted ourselves to fishing as best we could with everything that seemed likely to stop a fish and a lot of things that seemed unlikely, and remained to be proved otherwise. Farther up this same broad, slow-flowing river one of the great anglers of my boyhood still plied his rod. He had the weakness that has inhibited me all my life. He fished and fished again, believing that when he didn't fish he stood no chance. Admittedly, he fished in certain pools and at certain times of the day, but if he didn't take a fish he could say without fear of contradiction that he hadn't had the chance.

We consulted each evening and agreed that it was no wonder that the fish weren't taking. The water needed freshening. The pools were low and the chances were that the first time it really poured with rain the fish would go through on a marathon race. At the end of the first week we were reduced to fishing for pike and perch, pretending that we stood as good a chance of taking a salmon on the spinner when the water was almost lukewarm and the colour of whisky. The expert didn't condescend to fish for pike. He was low-watering, using finesse. It should have made a difference in the end, but it didn't; at least, not on that river while we were there.

At the end of the second week we talked of going along to the deep-freeze store and buying a fish that the netsmen had newly delivered. The nets were doing well, even if rumour had it that they were accepting one-and-sixpence a pound for their catch. The deep-freeze was almost packed to the doors and their critics were saying with disgust that soon they would be burying fish and pouring oil over them, as they had done a year or two earlier.

We caught nothing with great regularity, nothing that could be called a fish in Scotland. Friday was our final day on the river and during Thursday night it rained. I awoke to the sound of it drumming on a tin roof at the back of our little hotel. I could hear the river across the field there, where it cut through the rocks. It was already beginning to roar. I pictured it flowing in yellow-tinged froth, like the head on a glass of stout. It didn't seem to me that it would fine down in the course of a day to enable me to catch a fish down on the flats, but I could at least try. The salmon would surely be on the move.

We didn't venture out until after lunch. The fanatic wormers had been out all morning, taking baskets of good brown trout from the burns, as happy as otters or seals. The old hands waited. They would fish on Saturday, or perhaps on Monday. One or two incorrigible villains would sneak down on Sunday, but we had only one day, and it proved no better than the bright, sunny days and the midge-ridden evenings that had gone before. It was different, of course. The salmon went through with great regularity and the clegs wouldn't leave us alone for a minute. That was all.

My boyhood tutor, the old expert, caught two fish that day—on the next river. Instinct told him to go there and, in the middle of the afternoon, he took up his gear and went. At the best pool on this river, an association water, he took his place in a queue that finished up 12 men long. He was somewhere in the middle of the line. He used spinning gear and fished exactly the same water with the same spoon as seven of his neighbours. At the first pass he took a salmon of some 6 or 7lb. No one else among the 12 had a touch. At the second pass he took another. No one else had anything. In fact, no more fish were taken on the river that day! No fish had been taken for something like 10 weeks.

One man lucky and 10 or 11 frustrated? One man skilled and the rest not his equal? I know what I think. Perhaps I had better not say it. The experts would heap scorn upon me. All I'll say is I know where I am with a fish that rises to an Olive and belongs to one pool in the stream. Salmon fanatics are a determined lot, not unlike the fish that forces itself into the gill net when it could easily rise and swim over it!

November 1964   *Ian Niall*

November on Tweed

There can be but few salmon anglers who ever think of practising their favourite sport during November. Indeed, there are many I know who, because of the large numbers of red fish in the rivers at such a time, do not consider it even the correct thing to fish for salmon during October. The Tweed, however, is perhaps unique among British salmon rivers, for it is closed to salmon fishing only during December and January, and the fact that it gets continued runs of fresh fish throughout the season is perhaps difficult to comprehend.

On most rivers where a run of salmon is enjoyed, the spring fishing is always regarded as the best, the cream of the season. Indeed, this same label applies equally to Tweed, when from February onwards, to May, the river enjoys one of the finest spring runs of salmon. During the early and often bitter cold months, the fish tend to stay in the lower reaches, where beats such as Birgham, Sprouston, Hendersyde, Wark or Lennel often have vast stocks of fish to oblige the fortunate angler. As the water warms, so the fish move further upstream.

Depending on rainfall, mid-September sees a special type of fish waiting to run the Tweed, genuine autumn-run salmon, fish fresh from their rich summer feeding in the sea. These are fish which, during July and August, were still away out at sea, feeding and growing fat. It is not surprising, therefore, that genuine autumn-run fish are as fit as, maybe even fitter than, their spring cousins, and as they turn landward to get the scent of fresh water, their sexual urges are suddenly awakened. Perhaps they realise that there is still time to find a mate before the mantle of winter falls over the land.

With the first frosts of autumn, so the water temperatures cool and these fish are now committed to their freshwater pilgrimage. From September, right through to Christmas, they will run. As the waters cool, so the speed with which they move slows down. By mid-November, with anything like a normal autumn, the lower beats are once again full of late-run salmon, fresh and silvery fish with the sea-lice still on them, and with the exception of slightly more developed milt or ova, almost identical to their spring cousins.

Their spell in freshwater is going to be the shortest possible, for they could well spawn in the lower reaches and be back again at sea before the new season opens. But some fish may well wait until the early months of the new year before they finally find a mate. Even in February, with a new season open, it is still possible to catch fresh-run fish with milt or ova dripping from their bodies.

Often on Tweed they are labelled 'kippers' or 'baggots', depending upon their sex, but I suspect that they are not truly so, and if left might well find a mate and thus complete the cycle. Just as autumn fish in early spring are not uncommon, it is also possible to come across an early springer in November.

To the angler who does not want to put his tackle aside with the end of the spring run, there is a vast potential on Tweed and a chance of fresh-run fish in November.

Tactics to deal with such fish at this time of year have largely been dictated to the angler. Under the present ruling, nothing but fly fishing is allowed during the time when the netsmen are not permitted to fish. From the opening of the season, on February 1, fly-only is the rule until the fifteenth of the month. From then on, until the end of August, most legitimate forms of fishing are allowed.

Techniques for catching fish on fly during the hard months of autumn and spring have had to be modified quite alarmingly from normal greased-line methods. The big tube fly, fished on a heavy sinking line, has become standard procedure, but in the strict sense of the word it is hardly fly-fishing at all, for the 'flies' are often tied on long brass tubes, up to 3in long, and are so heavy that special techniques are required to cast them.

My favourite rig for autumn fishing consists of a 15ft tournament-type, fibreglass salmon rod. To fish with it for even an hour is a tiring process, so that when you have completed a day with it you will not need much rocking to sleep. The line is an exact half-portion of a 30yd GAAG sinking line spliced to 27lb monofil backing. With the 15yd head and a heavy fly it is just possible, under practical conditions, to aerialise this shooting head, but by coiling the monofil backing into the bottom of the boat, or around your left hand, it is quite easy to shoot a further 15yd of backing and thus make a good 30yd cast.

Long casting is essential for this type of fishing. The fish will no longer rise to the fly as they did back in the greased-line season. Instead, the fly has to be fished as low in the water as possible, just as one would do in early-season spinning for salmon. There will be little chance to mend the line, but even so it is just possible immediately after the cast has been completed. Casts should be made fairly square and a small portion of line shot at the time of the mend to help get the fly down before the strong current puts too much belly in the line.

Only by making long casts will you make the fly fish at any worthwhile depth, for with short casts the thick line causes too much water drag, and thus makes the fly fish too high in the water.

Many newcomers to this type of fishing, even expert, greased-line fishermen, find the technique difficult. The fly and casting-head have, in fact, to be regarded purely as a weight at the end of the rod. Any attempts to cast in the traditional style will almost certainly bring disappointment. The action with the fly-rod must be very slow, and a pause must be made in the back cast until the full weight of fly and line is felt pulling at the rod-tip. Only then should the forward cast be made, well up into the air, clear of the water-line, in order to give time for the backing to be shot before the fly reaches the water.

Fishing thus there will be many false alarms as your fly scrapes over rocks and obstructions in the bottom of the river. It is not quite the same as getting hung up with a spinning bait, and for the first few times you are quite entitled to think that a salmon has taken your fly. Normally, however, when the fly is taken, there is not much doubt about it. A firm, strong pull is the usual effect and I rarely bother to feed any slack line before raising the rod-tip and driving the treble home. In the cold waters of November the fish may not fight with the verve and sparkle of a late-spring or summer fish. Instead they bore relentlessly in an effort to shake the hook and, as the gaff is not allowed, the fish are usually netted by the boatman.

If you are fishing without a gillie you must either beach your fish or tail it out yourself. It all adds interest and makes the game even more exciting, particularly if you happen to have one of the big late-run fish at the end of the line.

Unhappily, at the present time, salmon disease is altering the entire conception of normal autumn fishing. But with the end of the disease, there should be good days again on Tweed in November.

November 1968   *Arthur Oglesby*

The light touch . . . when playing salmon

The angler who counts himself as a duffer when it comes to throwing a straight line, or fails to keep his fly from walloping the rocks on a back cast, need not despair. If he can hook, play and land his salmon

197

Last days on the Tweed: winter settles on the riverside trees as a salmon-fisher
makes the most of a short late-November day on the Nest fishings at Peel Bridge

within a reasonable time, and that without fuss, whistle-blowing or
help from friends, then he has nothing to worry about; but if he still
hankers after a smooth, professional style, he may rest assured that
it will come eventually.

However, this happy state of affairs is likely to elude the fisherman
unless he is prepared to give a little thought to the control of his
fish after it has been hooked, and thus avoid the use of strong-arm
tactics, except in cases of dire necessity.

That there is nothing new in this suggestion is borne out by the
writers of old-time textbooks, who always made a point of quoting

the runaway salmon. Readers were adjured to screw up their courage, drop their rod-points and give the fugitive its head. This allowed it to turn upstream once again and permit its respiratory organs to function correctly. It was an excellent piece of advice, but, for the timid, a difficult one to implement.

The first time I met one of these tearaway fish was while fishing the Spey, more than 30 years ago. Without the slightest warning the rod was nearly dragged from my fingers and the reel began to butt like a mad thing, and all of 75yd of line had been pulled off before I could bring myself to do the right thing, and let the fish run free.

The reactions of hooked salmon do not seem to change, and this simple example, in which advantage is taken of their inability to remain facing downstream without drowning, is as true today as it was a century ago. That it is not easy to give a salmon its head is readily admitted, but I suggest it is well worth the effort, because it could well be the first step towards a way of fishing that allows the angler a certain amount of control over his quarry and cuts out that feckless pulling and hauling which not infrequently goes on until the unfortunate salmon rolls over and dies in its tracks.

This method offers nothing new, but merely exploits the vulnerability of certain reactions of hooked salmon, while conforming to the belief that the place from which to bring pressure to bear on them is downstream. For ease of reference I have divided the method into four phases: hooking, walking-up, general playing, and the last phase.

The reactions of a salmon immediately after it has been hooked show no definite pattern, except that there is usually a display of aquatics followed by a short period of calm when, it is presumed, the fish is trying to rid itself of the lure. This is the time for the angler to take control, and his first move should be to walk his salmon up to the top of the pool (or as far as possible), thus giving himself plenty of room in which to play it, and that from the downstream position.

The practice of walking-up salmon must be as old as the hills, yet it is often rediscovered by contributors to the angling press. I had the experience of being walked-up myself on one occasion. This particular fish moved so quickly that I was unable to keep up with it and fell heavily on the wet and slippery bank, whereupon it showed its good manners by waiting until I was on my feet before moving off again. Incidentally, it showed another side of its character later on by wiping my eye and departing without a backward glance.

The thrill of having a salmon follow like a dog on a leash is real indeed. Some need coaxing and move slowly with frequent stops, while others, like the one I have mentioned, are in such a hurry that control is lost. With care and gentle pressure they may be persuaded to go through the drill twice, occasionally three times, but sooner or later they wake up to the fact that something is wrong and go off like a packet of crackers. The angler has to turn his back on his fish, hold his rod over the river, and place a couple of fingers lightly on the reel drum, as a precaution against this sudden awakening.

It should be clearly understood that these remarks refer only to newly-hooked fish. Any attempt to walk them about later on is likely to result in torn hook-holds or broken lines.

Unfortunately, few river banks are free of obstructions, and it is seldom that the whole length of a pool can be utilised. Nevertheless, additional distance can be gained by the application of upstream side-stress, which merely requires that the rod be swung upstream and over the bank. This has the effect of throwing the fish off course. Its immediate reaction is to use its tail to straighten up, with the result that it is driven further up-river.

The angler, having reached the limit of his walk, must now step smartly downstream to a point some 10 to 20yd below his fish, maintaining a uniform pressure throughout this rather tricky *volte-face*.

With the first two phases accomplished, the angler is ideally placed to exert the maximum strain on his quarry, which has now to contend with the current, pressure from the rod when held in the normal manner, and, what must be equally tiring, from spells of upstream side-stress. Further, if the salmon can be persuaded to go through the walking-up process once more, then it will have little steam left for general play, and the last phase cannot be long delayed.

The reactions of salmon during the run of play are legion, and quite outside the scope of this article, so I will confine myself to just one which, in its initial stages, brings humiliation to the fisherman and hilarity to the unsympathetic onlooker.

This is the salmon that swims doggedly to the other side of the river and, come what may, refuses to return, and there is precious little comfort to be obtained from the knowledge that once the movement has been started, it is not cussedness but the pull from the waterlogged line that accounts for the fish's strange behaviour. It would be an understatement to say that control has been lost, for, on the face of it, any action on the part of the angler may cause the sunk line to become snagged or the hook-hold to be torn out.

Fortunately for us, the salmon has a habit of jumping when caught in this predicament; and it has been found that if the rod-point can be dropped before the fish leaves the water, then for a short time it seems to lose all sense of direction.

It would be reasonable to assume that this herculean task would require a certain amount of limbering up, and I believe it is this that can be felt right up the line and down to the hands. This is the cue for the angler to drop his rod-point and regain control. He can either walk straight back from the river, towing his fish behind him, or stand fast and pump it back as quickly as possible. The decision depends on the height and state of the bank. In my experience, the salmon usually regains its wits somewhere about the middle of the river, but by this time the initiative should have passed to the angler.

In dealing with the last stage of the encounter, I am reminded of a memorable forenoon when I hooked and lost three salmon, all around the 20lb mark. The river was high, the current strong, and having dragged them upstream to within a few yards of me, I realised, with a sinking heart, that I could do no more. Whatever I did brought me no nearer to them, and in due course, they all slipped back into the stream with broken hook-holds.

Now, having the luck to fish a beat that consists of five little pools, all of which possess small backwaters at their lower ends, there are no problems. Every fish is walked up and eventually taken down to one of the backwaters for the last rites. Even these can be carried through in an orderly fashion, as the banks have been cleared for easy access.

The reactions of the salmon at this time reflect the skill of the fisherman. To bustle it into slack water while it still has sufficient strength to get out again is asking for trouble, bearing in mind that both tackle and hook-hold may already be strained to the limit. On the other hand, for the fish to have died *en route* indicates a lack of skill and a show of timidity on the part of the angler, for we owe it to this courageous opponent that the encounter shall not be long-drawn-out and that its end be swift and certain.

I know of nothing more nauseating than to watch a salmon gasp out its last moments in a flurry of scales, while its victor saunters about the shingle looking for a large enough stone wherewith to finish it off.

There is hardly any reaction that cannot be countered by some means, other than brute force and unimaginativeness, to use a polite phrase. The substitution of a light touch for the deathlike grip on rod and reel affords considerable satisfaction in itself, and when coupled with an effective method of dealing with these reactions, gives salmon fishing a much wider aspect.

August 1970   *Douglas Iron*

The Tay again

Too often in the North, winter lingers on into April and sudden summer comes to us in May. Spring, therefore, is inclined to be more an attitude of mind than a season.

With some of us, indeed, spring arrives each year, despite the weather, on January 15, when the Tay salmon season opens. I have beached my first fish on more than one occasion by sliding it over a fringe of ice into the snow, and I have struggled waist-deep through drifts to reach the pools. But always it is spring, vibrant spring, in the mind.

Every year, of course, does not give us a start in snow and ice. The weather is like the fish at the opening—unpredictable! And there have been opening days when the sun shone from a cloudless sky, when the Tay was bright blue and at a level, though not a temperature, for greased-line fishing.

What will it be this year? I will be quite happy if the start is in drifting snowflakes, for Tay salmon often take well when it snows. Frost is the thing that can spoil my opening, for I like to fish from the bank with moderate tackle, and when ice forms on the line and fills the rings a complete jam takes place, and I have to pack up. This often happens in the early fishing.

It is wise to stop when ice begins to form, but on one occasion I persisted after freezing started. And I hooked a salmon. Very soon the rings filled up and it looked as if a break must follow. However, I put the whole rod in the running water and let the fish go where it wished until the ice melted. By repeating this immersion every few minutes, the rings were kept clear, and eventually the fish was landed. But by the time I had killed it the reel was frozen solid!

Practically all early Tay-fishing is done from boats, the particular method used being known as harling. And although heavy tackle is used, this harling is a very successful way of fishing. It allows the bait both to hang over the fish and to drop downstream from time to time in a way that the bank spinner is unable to copy.

Fishing from the bank, I can usually hold my own in friendly competition with the boat when warmer conditions come along, but in the cold waters at the beginning the boat almost always wins. This, I am sure, is due to the hanging presentation of the bait to the somewhat lethargic, early fish.

Sprats are the usual baits in the spring, and it is interesting that when the water is very cold the silver sprat is almost invariably the killing one, whereas after the water has warmed up the gold sprat is taken and the silver ignored. This has been noticeable over the years.

When I first went to the Tay I followed the old advice to search the deep holes for early fish in cold conditions, and to rake the bottom with the bait. As the years went on, however, I learned better from experience, and my sport improved.

Salmon never lie in deep holes. The best spring lies I know are where the water is 6 or 8ft deep. And cold or mild, the fish will be there. If an angler hooks a salmon in a very deep pool, he may be sure that the fish has followed his lure from the shelving edge of the pool or from a rock cleft at reasonable depth.

The spring lies I know have one thing in common—the current is smooth-flowing and the surface unbroken. It is only when the water warms that the fish seem to move into broken streams, and, of course, in high summer the rougher the stream, the better do the salmon like it.

I feel sure it must have been a tackle-maker with an eye to business who started the idea of bumping the bottom when spinning for early salmon! At all events I have found that it pays better (both in fish and in tackle) to keep the spinner up a bit. The most effective position for the bait in spring is somewhere just below mid-water.

Almost invariably salmon take—either bait or fly—on an upward curve, and while an early bait should be quite near the fish, and travelling slowly, too, my feeling is that it will be taken more readily—and more naturally—if it is hanging slightly above the resting salmon.

Even in the chill days of early spring it is worth casting on into the dusk so long as frost permits. As wild duck flight each evening, so do salmon move restlessly about the pools as daylight fails. And many a dour day has brought its reward among the last casts.

More than once I have watched salmon, as dusk was beginning, swimming slowly round the edge of a pool. These fish showed none of the excitement of running salmon; they seemed simply to be taking a quiet evening swim as we might take an evening stroll. It seems to me that this evening swim is a token movement among salmon that are not, for one reason or other, on the run.

Once on the Tay I gave up fishing as the rise of a bright moon coincided with the dusk. Both my host, who was harling, and I had been unsuccessful all day, but as I approached his pool I saw that he was playing a fish. After landing it he began to put out the baits again, but before he had completed that job another fish took. And this was repeated three times before the salmon went off the take. He landed three clean fish and two kelts in quick succession. By the time he had finished it was pure moonlight; and that pool had been fished earlier in the day without a touch.

I may say we have tried this pool in similar conditions since then, but the success of that particular night has not been repeated. It does show, however, that the belief that moonlight is bad for fishing is not always correct.

So we look forward to another opening day, wondering if it will be in conditions of frost, snow or flood. But whatever is in store matters little so long as we can go out again with the rod and try for an early springer, fresh in from the sea, with his back of pigeon-blue and burnished silver on his sides.

January 1956   *Ian Wood*

Summer tactics on the Welsh Dee

Last year was a particularly good one on the Welsh Dee. The lower beats fished well in the early season and a good run of fish arrived later further up-river.

In common with others, I have always had my share of spring fish, but until a few years ago I never had much success in summer. Discussions on the subject led me to believe that I am one of the many who have never made much of a profit with the orthodox greased-line method. I have read most of the available books on the subject and listened to a great deal of advice. The fish, however, rarely wanted to do business. The only floating-line expert I have known was my father, but unfortunately he died at a time when my main interest was in fixed-spool reels.

I soon began to wonder whether the parts of the Welsh Dee which I fish lent themselves to the classic Cairnton style. I almost need to wet my ears to get within reasonable casting distance of many of the lies, and my ability to control 25 to 30yd of floating line while up to my armpits in the water, is, to put it mildly, less than indifferent. Possibly the main drawback is a slight lack of confidence in the method. I do not like to think of my fly drifting like a dead thing an inch or two under water. I prefer fondly to imagine my hook on an even keel, rising and falling in the water according to the strength of the current.

During the past few seasons I have used the orthodox greased line less and less. I continue to fish the normal spring method, but with much lighter tackle. I use rods of 11 and 12ft, smaller, sparser flies, and obviously finer casts. This method has produced fish, but has many drawbacks. It is impossible to control a sunk line and thus regulate the speed of the fly. Of course, one can lead with the rod, but this is not always enough. Furthermore, one does not always want the fly near the bed of the river.

I therefore greased all but the last 10 or 12ft of my line and started to get the best of both worlds. I could now mend and lead my line, thus controlling the speed of my fly. A further dividend was the ability to control the depth at which it fished by alternating the angle of my cast and/or the size of my mend.

Having taught myself the method it was now necessary to work out the tactics. It seems to me that these summer fish soon get bored if they are shown a fly too often. Any attempt to 'force-feed' is fatal. A salmon-fisherman does not have to be a marathon runner, and constantly pestering a rising fish may not stop it rising, but will generally ruin one's chances of getting it.

One July day I was fishing at Erbistock. When I was halfway down the pool a small fish rose in a neck. I fished the pool out, put on a smaller fly, stood well above the lie and cast to the fish. I showed it the fly twice, but it showed no interest. I reeled in, sat on the bank, and shared a piece of cake with my dog. Everything indicated that this fish should take. It looked fresh and was in a good taking lie.

I walked into the river again, cast well above the fish and mended my line in order to sink the fly on its far side. When I judged it in the right place, I mended the floating part of my line downstream and, as the current caught hold, the fly was brought past the fish rising to the surface. It took it like a starving tiger. Later in the day I had another small fish from the same place. It's funny how these small fish seem to lie in pairs.

During last season I accounted for about a dozen fish with this induced-take method (sorry, Major Kite). Possibly, as the fly fishes the lie rising to the surface, the fish thinks it is trying to escape and some predatory instinct is aroused. Anyway, it is only the empirical which concerns me.

One August Saturday I was fishing near Corwen. The river was low and the day fairly bright. There was a fish rising in the run into the bottom pool, but though I tried it half-a-dozen different times, it wouldn't play. As I was fishing down to the fish once more, a pair of mallard flew up the river and I turned to watch them. Despite my polarising glasses I was half blinded by the sun.

Then it struck me. The fly was coming to the fish out of the sun and therefore it would have a poor view of it until too late. I cast my fly into the slack water on my own side of the run. Pulling a couple of yards of line off my reel, I made a prodigious mend out over the stream. I held my rod-point high and watched the fly move into the current from my own side. Nothing doing. I tried once again and I was into the fish.

I have since used a combination of these tactics to show my fly to some fish that I have been previously unable to reach. Standing as near as possible directly upstream of the lies, I have cast downstream to the slack water on the far side. Then, holding my rod-point high, I have stripped off line until the current has taken my fly as far down as I needed it. I have then made a downstream mend which brought

Nearly home. . . . It's late in the season and a salmon takes the falls at Killiecrankie
on the Perthshire Garry

my fly slowly through the stream. This accounted for two fish in 15 minutes which I would not have got any other way.

I have no wish to denigrate the Wood style of fishing and have the greatest admiration for those who can consistently catch fish with it. It just doesn't seem to suit me. I have more confidence in this sunk-tip method, and I suppose that's what really counts.

May 1967   *S. J. Diggory*

Thoughts on autumn salmon

There are those who hold forth on the iniquity of catching salmon in the autumn, when these fish have well-developed spawn in them. Such critics apparently do not know that the autumn salmon stays in the sea until its spawn is nearly mature. The feeding in the sea is so rich that the spawn is grown without the fish having to use up any of its tissues in the process. Because of this an autumn fish, if fresh run, is in excellent condition, having as much fat, or curd, as the best springer.

As these fish are never in our rivers until the autumn, I can only presume that those who despise the autumn fish, and the autumn fisherman, are suggesting that these big salmon should not be fished for at all. Perhaps, however, those who disapprove imagine that autumn fish will come up the rivers at some other time of year, and such a mistaken assumption would be an adequate reason for objecting to autumn fishing.

Those who have had practical experience on a good autumn river can remember many a hard fight with big, late salmon, when the reel screeched, and the water hissed as the line cut through the surface. One cannot forget that slow, heavy draw as the fish takes hold. It has a different feel on the big rod and heavy line, somehow more thrilling and satisfactory even than the pull on a greased line and lighter tackle.

I am all in favour of fishing for autumn salmon and can remember many good days with the fly on the Tweed, and on other late rivers.

The fish play as well as any springers. If legitimate fishing is ever unsporting, then surely catching springers with a sprat in cold water in February would be a good example. I have often experienced this kind of fishing, which can be boring, requiring little or no skill, and providing the minimum of sport. The tackle and hooks are coarse, and when the water is really cold the very best springer will not run off many yards of line, being content to bore about close at hand, until exhausted.

Add to the poor performance of the half-frozen springer the discomfort of cold hands and surely it is preferable to catch the wild, dashing autumn fish, in comparatively clement weather.

I should perhaps point out here that I have been discussing proper autumn salmon, not back-end springers. The springer (unlike the autumn fish) grows its spawn in freshwater, and having not only had to do this, but also to keep itself alive without proper feeding, is in poor condition by the autumn, and is in consequence not worth catching. Because of this it is essential to make sure that the river you fish, from the beginning of September to the end of the season, has a run of real autumn fish.

For example, the Spey does not have any appreciable autumn run, and the autumn runs in the Tay and the Dee are also negligible, so that these rivers are not, in my opinion, worth fishing after the summer. It is possible that those disapproving of autumn fishing have such rivers in mind, not having fished a proper autumn water.

One might expect that the size of the fish, in the rivers that have autumn runs, would be in proportion to the size of the river. This, however, does not follow. The Don, which is a smaller river than the Tweed, has a larger proportion of big fish of 30lb and over than the Tweed had when it was an autumn water. The North Esk, which again is smaller than the Don, has many autumn fish of 25lb and more.

As these fish have grown their spawn in the sea, they are much nearer the spawning time when they enter the river than are the fresh-run springers. Because of this they have a greater urge to travel up to the spawning grounds, and so do not often settle sufficiently long to take well if the river is running much above its normal height. These fish will not lie over a dirty river-bottom and are more particular about this than are the springers. If the river is too low for them to travel, they will clear a lie for themselves, but if they can continue upstream, an unclean river-bottom may make them decide to do so. Naturally, fish travelling up may and do lie in the places that have already been cleaned by earlier fish.

In years of drought these fish will force their way up at night, travelling over shallows with their backs out of water. Once on a September evening, when fishing for finnock in the Sea Pool of the North Esk, I saw a shoal of big fish go over the ford which was only about 5in deep. Seeing them push their way up making a terrific commotion, with much noisy thrashing of great tails, was a sight to remember.

Autumn fish generally take a sunk fly fairly well. The newer the fish, and the nearer to the sea, the bigger the fly should be, coming down to smaller sizes progressively as one ascends the river, where the water in consequence becomes smaller and shallower, and the fish staler. Although they will generally take a fly reasonably well, they will also take a small spinning bait.

If the weather is cold, both fly and bait should be fished slowly. In warm weather, or with the water temperature above normal, a faster fly or bait may, and often does, give better results.

The cock fish assumes a red colour as his spawning plumage, and this has nothing to do with the time he has been in freshwater. He frequently leaves the sea with his red colouring, and it is not uncommon to catch a really red cock fish with sea-lice on him. This colouring is to please and attract the female and serves no other purpose. It is obvious, therefore, that fish like this colour and that is presumably why flies with red in them are good killers in the autumn. The cock fish, with his predilection for reddish flies, seems to be as pleased with his colour scheme as is the hen.

Like the fly, a spinning bait should have some orange-red on it.

A small spoon, with similarly coloured tinsel-paper glued on the concave side with copal varnish, may do well. As with a fly and spinning bait, these spoons should be fished slowly and evenly in cold water, and at a faster steady speed if the water is warm. A bait the size of a number 4 Phantom is generally large enough, even in a big, coloured water.

The fresh-run female autumn fish is a bar of silver, with a brown back, and has all the bloom of a fresh-run springer. It is only after spawning that the backs of both the cock and hen fish become blue in colour. At the same time the red spawning plumage of the cock, and the rather drab grey of the spawned female, begin to resemble chromium plating in preparation for their return to salt water.

September 1956   *G. P. R. Balfour-Kinnear*